Just a Little From the Top ...

Reflections From the Keyboard and Beyond

RODERICK ELMS

The Choir Press

Body text typeset in 11pt Palatino

First published in the United Kingdom in 2020 by
The Choir Press

ISBN 978-1-78963-150-0

*This book is dedicated to the memory of my
wonderful parents, without whose devoted
support and encouragement life would
have been very different.*

Mum and Dad (late '40s)

Mum and Dad in my garden at Bethell Avenue (mid-'80s)

I would like to thank everyone who has offered me encouragement and support in collecting and writing these memoirs. Particular thanks go to my wife, Joanna, and our son, Matthew, for their enduring patience – I could not have done this without their help and support. Special thanks go to Stephen Bell, Peter Bullett, Nicola Harries, Adrian Levine, Andrew Neilson, Kate Quarry, Stephen Quigley, Martin Roberts, Claire Selby, Janet Snowman, Bramwell Tovey, Derek Wright and Martin Yates.

Roderick Elms, June 2020

Antiphon

Prelude

"You the organist?" screeched a small lady of mature years.

"Yes," I replied, very aware that she was blocking my passage to the organ in London's Royal Albert Hall for the second half of the concert.

"Well, I don't *know* you. Anyway, I don't like it; it's too big."

"Excuse me?" I replied.

"The organ – it's too big," she continued. "I've had a go, and it's too big." With that, she wandered off to her seat.

Now, it's not uncommon for people to show an interest in this iconic instrument, and it's always a pleasure to talk about the organ and its 9,999 pipes (hold that thought, as it's usually the next question to be asked). The idea that this lady had managed to get past the security rope to the organ console, swing her legs over the organ bench, find the *On* button and make some sounds, all without apparently attracting the attention of the hall's staff, rather caught my imagination. Quite a remarkable feat! However, when I reached the organ, the bench had certainly been moved …

A by-product of this year's (2020) appalling coronavirus crisis was providing time to give further thought to the idea of writing down some anecdotes. I've been encouraged to do this for some years, especially after past experiences or funny situations have come up in conversation with friends and colleagues. However, it soon became clear that I couldn't find an obvious distinction between memoirs and autobiography, and while it wasn't my intention to write much biographical detail, some was needed to put certain experiences into context.

These memoirs contain a mixture of emotions, nothing deep or profound. Most are very happy; some, not so happy; others are just memories. Sometimes we are lucky in life; at other times, not so lucky – life perhaps not treating us as we would hope to be treated. For some years, I have been keeping brief notes on my phone, but it was the reality of the current lockdown that provided the incentive to make a proper start.

The plan was to simply write a few pages of anecdotes, but when reality set in, I found it hard not to put many things into the chronological context of my wider life, and the project grew! I hope that those who offered me encouragement won't be disappointed. Apart from my work in professional music-making, I have written a little about my early life, my education, and student days at the Royal Academy of Music. I've also included some of my experiences living in the London Borough of Redbridge, and the huge impact the music service in that borough had, not just on *my* musical future, but also that of a great many others.

I always considered my first 'professional' engagement to have been in March 1978; therefore, the majority of this book relates to my work as a keyboard player and composer from that time, spanning a period of more than forty years. I appreciate that not all of this will interest everyone – to paraphrase, you can't interest everyone all of the time – and you will not offend me if you skip over the occasional section. I've not included any specific coda signs, but if you feel the need to 'Jump to Coda', it starts on page 174. I've included quite a few photographs – I like photos, and they can help to give the narrative a bit of clarity.

These memoirs have been a long time coming – some might say not long enough! I hope that they will be of interest and maybe give something of an insight into the mysteries of the music profession – one that offers so many wonderful rewards and friendships and to which it's a privilege to contribute.

Family holiday (mid-'50s)

1 – Early Years

"Just a little from the top" might well be the most common – yet unintentional – untruth to be uttered by conductors to the orchestral musicians sitting in front of them, and no doubt hanging on to their every word. I'm sure they don't mean to play the whole piece through again, but ...

I imagine that for many people, the road to achieving a goal can be similarly paved with good intentions that can, ultimately, be frustrated. And so it may be that my well-intended plan to produce a concise summary of the funny and not-so-funny experiences from more than forty years working in the music profession may not have succeeded in all respects, being rather longer than anticipated!

You could say that life as I now know it began with a huge sneeze – a substantial explosion, but not one that was infectious, at least not in the generally perceived way. This was a full orchestral sneeze – one that infected me with a bug for orchestral playing. If you can manage to read beyond this chapter, you will discover how. However, I need to rewind a few years before reaching for my handkerchief. When I was two, our family moved from Aldeburgh Road North (close to Seven Kings, near Ilford in Essex) to Ridgeway Gardens – in a small area near Ilford called Redbridge, which was to give its name to a new London borough following the reorganisation of the boroughs in 1965. Redbridge embraced the old Essex towns of Ilford, Wanstead and Woodford (n.b. Seven Kings will become crucial to a project later in life).

I started to have piano lessons when I was five – not as early as my brilliant wife Joanna, of course, but still the earliest that was allowed by any of the teachers in our immediate locality. This must have been coincident with my starting at Redbridge Primary School, which by good fortune was in the road immediately

At home in Ridgeway Gardens, Redbridge Primary School in background

opposite our house – barely a minute's walk and therefore maximising time at home to do more interesting things. That said, sometimes I would walk out of school into smog and couldn't see our house barely fifty yards away. This was quite some time before the crucial Clean Air Act of 1968 came into place, prohibiting the emission of dark smoke from chimneys.

During my time at Redbridge, I was given all sorts of musical encouragement, including accompanying the hymns in assembly and playing for school concerts. I was also allowed to indulge my considerable interest in all things electronic – wiring up the stage lighting for productions and designing a new PA system for sports day. In retrospect, I'm sure this would be unthinkable these days, with the current obsession for Health and Safety – which seemingly doesn't allow people to learn from their own mistakes. I also appreciated the opportunity these escapades afforded to avoid lessons! I was in charge of the school projector when films were to be shown, as well as operating the slide-strip projector in my last term for the new French lessons – I can still hear the first words, "*C'est ma maison.*" It's interesting to note that our son Matthew has been learning basic French for more than two years now in his primary school as well as having regular homework in

Mum and Dad's wedding, Goodmayes (May 1949)

maths and English – something we never did 'back in the day'.

My mum, Hazel, was born in March 1923 in Ilford. She had a difficult upbringing, and her parents divorced, which was relatively unusual at the time. Her mother's obsession with her new husband was at the expense of the children (Mum and her two brothers, Don and Des), who were rather left to fend for themselves. For quite a while, Mum lived with her grandmother, whom she adored. When in her early teens,

Mum (mid-late '40s)

Dad (mid-late '40s)

she regularly went on tour, learning to dance and act (on the job). She also developed considerable skills as a ballet dancer, which she also employed whilst working for ENSA (Entertainment National Services Association) during the war, entertaining the troops in Europe. Mum appeared in musicals both in London as well as in provincial theatres.

Dad (Jimmy) was born in January 1925 in Byfleet, Surrey. He had two older brothers (John and Peter) and a younger sister (Janet) – all Dad's family was from Surrey. My parents met whilst Mum was in a show in South Wales and Dad was in the RAF, and they married in All Saints Church in Goodmayes, Essex, on the 28th May 1949. After leaving the RAF, Dad trained as a heating engineer in Norwich, where he lived with Mum following their marriage.

It wasn't long before they both returned to Ilford, Dad eventually joining a building company, where he acted as a quantity surveyor, becoming a director and contracts manager and overseeing many large projects for HM Government. These included several of the post-war underground nuclear shelters built around the country, about which he was sworn to secrecy. I always chuckle when I drive into Ongar and see the brown sign proudly indicating the way to the 'Secret Nuclear Bunker'!

Dad with Penny and Noddy (early '60s)

My parents developed a keen interest in breeding and showing boxer dogs, and we would periodically have a full litter of puppies in the kennel at the far end of the garden. They could be quite vocal, and I'm not sure the early morning alarm was appreciated by our immediate neighbours. Most of the puppies were passed to other owners, but we did keep two special ones – Noddy and Penny. Mum and Dad enjoyed showing the dogs, and we would regularly leave the house at an unearthly hour to drive up the A1 for a dog show in Leeds or some other far-flung city. This, of course, was before the birth of Britain's first motorway – the M1, in 1959.

For most of my life, I remember my father bringing his building knowledge and DIY skills to bear on our house, which he would enthusiastically pull apart to install new heating or electrical circuits. As a small boy, I would regularly be sent (willingly) under the floorboards to help with routing pipes and cables. It was another world under there and one that was hugely exciting at that age. I'm sure that this, together with the arrival of an electronics kit one Christmas, led to my lifelong passion for matters technical and building electronic equipment.

I understand that I was called Roderick as my parents wanted a slightly longer and not too common first name to complement the short surname. Too long for some, as a child I was usually called Roddy, but now it's generally Rod, although as friends will know, I have a serious dislike of 'Rod Elms'! Apparently, had my gender been assigned differently, I would have been a Penelope. Although an only child, I was fortunate to have three cousins (Clare, Lydia, and Clive, who was somewhat younger) living next-door-but-one with my godparents, my mum's brother Des and his wife, Beryl. We spent a great deal of time playing together.

Mum's siblings: Dad, Mum, Des Weston's second wife Joan, Don Weston and Des Weston (whose first wife, Beryl, passed away while still quite young). Don was married to Barbara.

Dad's siblings: John Elms, Dad, Peter Elms and Janet Nowell (née Elms). John married Nora, Peter married Stella and Janet married Colin.

I remember my mum playing the piano, and I gather I was trying to emulate her from a very early age, picking out tunes (I'm told that's what they were) as soon as I was able to clamber onto the piano stool. My father played the bugle, although that particular musical talent skipped a generation to our son Matthew. My father's mother was also a good pianist, and she would entertain us when we visited the Elms' family home in New Haw (ultimately demolished to make way for the new M25). She also gave me a first edition copy of *Carols for Choirs* back in the sixties (the green one) – a copy I still treasure and use every year, despite its attempts to self-destruct.

Meanwhile, piano lessons with Freda (Freddy) Ellinger were a pleasure, and I believe progress was quite swift. She taught through pure enthusiastic encouragement, a remarkable ability to instil self-confidence, and also a system of reward by grading lessons as Good, Very Good or Excellent. Three 'Excellents' resulting, if I remember correctly, with the reward of 6d (that's old pennies) – this was the 1950s! I always looked forward to my weekly walk to Somersby Gardens, and I think I was pretty good at practice during the intervening days, although I'm sure I had to receive periodic 'encouragement'.

My parents loved entertaining, in both Ridgeway Gardens and their later home in Tillotson Road, Ilford. They regularly hosted parties which, of course, were obligatory after concerts. At Christmas, the house was packed with both the immediate and extended family – a tradition that seemed to become accepted as the status quo by everyone involved.

Early musical life involved the usual round of local musical festivals and other competitions. By the time I was nine, Freddy had become a family friend. However, she decided, most generously, that it might be in my best interests to move to a teacher who could help me develop in ways that she couldn't. This was Cimbro Martin, at the Guildhall School of Music and Drama (GSMD), at that time in Blackfriars, London, and arrangements were made for me to study there with him as a Junior Exhibitioner. I don't remember much about him except that he seemed very tall, always wore a bow tie, and would sometimes come in very late for our half-hour lessons, telling me that twenty minutes with him was worth half-an-hour with anyone else! The old GSMD building was directly opposite the City of London School for Boys (CLS), where I was to study a few years later.

This new arrangement meant trips to London every Saturday morning, and with this came opportunities to play solos in recitals, as well as concertos with the student orchestra – Mozart K. 449 and Beethoven's Second (actually No. 1, but apparently things became a little confused with Ludwig's cataloguing). It was here that I experienced a pipe organ for the first time close-up. I was fascinated and set about arranging the Grieg Concerto for piano and organ, in lieu of orchestra. Co-students included the respected orchestral leader and solo violinist, Marcia Crayford, as well as her sister, Helen Crayford (also with Cimbro Martin) – a vivacious and fun person who also plays the trumpet – her party piece being to play the trumpet while simultaneously accompanying herself on the piano!

Life was good at Redbridge Primary School, but eventually the time came to take the 11+ (compulsory in those days) and ultimately accept the place I had been offered at the City of London School. I remember my interview there with the headmaster, Dr Arthur Barton, when I was asked about the books I read. I came away with the distinct feeling that he wasn't impressed with my reply!

With Dad in the garden of Aldborough Road (1952)

With my cousin Clare (mid-'50s)

2 – Big School

In September 1963, I took my first steps inside the City of London School for Boys as a pupil. I can't say that it wasn't intimidating, but life gradually became more comfortable. On my first day, we were told our school houses (no Sorting Hat here), and I was assigned to Seeley. At the end of the day, we had to go to house meetings and having found the room, and successfully hidden myself in a corner at the back, I was mortified to hear someone come in and call out very loudly, "Elms? Is Elms here?"

Apparently, I had been misplaced and should have been in Mortimer house. There was nothing for it but to own up and walk the length of the room to the door – it felt like an eternity!

Our first music lesson was with the assistant director of music, Roy Wilkinson, who was quite a demanding and controlling personality. He played us Ravel's *Boléro* and expected that this class of eleven-year-olds would be able to identify all the orchestral solos as they appeared. I

City of London School, Victoria Embankment site. Now Head Office of J.P. Morgan.

remember him being rather rattled that his expectations were not fulfilled, although no doubt this was not the first time he'd tried this idea. Roy gave me many opportunities for solo performance, both on special occasions in school as well as outside recitals, and although my relationship with him was sometimes testing, I will always appreciate that generosity of spirit.

The school I knew was an imposing building situated on Victoria Embankment, close to Blackfriars Bridge – for years, a photo of the school was seen rising with great regularity from the River Thames during the London Weekend Television station caption. The school had originally opened in Milk Street in 1837 but eventually outgrew its premises. The new building in Blackfriars was opened in 1883, and the school remained there until 1986, moving to its present location at the north end of the Millennium Bridge. The main building was on four floors, with the science labs situated mostly on the fourth. There was a climb of one hundred steps to reach the music block perched on the fifth, somewhat reminiscent of a ship's bridge with (from 1965) Capt. Wilkinson in command!

I hadn't been at the school for long when it made the evening papers – some wag had decided to fly a bra from one of the flagpoles. Despite the towers each side of the building being easily accessible from the gallery in the Great Hall, I remember being quite impressed that anyone could have that level of courage to carry out such a grave misdemeanour. I have no idea whether they were ever caught.

A great attraction for me at my new school was the presence of a pipe organ placed to the side of the gallery in the Great Hall. This was not a large instrument, but it had considerable allure to a twelve-year-old. It was also a curiosity in that its blower (to supply wind to the pipes) was the only electrical device left in the City of London to need the old DC (direct current) mains supply and therefore had its own power station in the vicinity of Fleet Street. In the morning, the school choir would sit in the gallery and lead the singing of the morning hymn, and the organ would usually be played by one of the school's music staff.

Here I taught myself to play the organ, getting to school at around 8:10am every day and sitting alone in the Great Hall, obsessing over J.S. Bach's (attrib.) ubiquitous Toccata and Fugue in D minor. Later, the school was to have a brand new instrument constructed by the respected firm of organ builders, J. W. Walker & Sons. That instrument still exists today and sits proudly at the back of the stage in the new school building. The organ had actually been designed for this location, although, for a few years, it sat, seemingly perilously, in the shallow gallery of the old building.

The school Music Society regularly organised outings, and one of these was to the Walker factory, which, at the time, was in Ruislip. One of the instruments we saw being constructed in the factory was that for the new Metropolitan Cathedral in Liverpool, and I believe that the installation was completed with just two days to go before the opening of the cathedral. Following a downturn in its fortunes, the firm of Walkers subsequently moved to Brandon in Suffolk, where it was revitalised and managed by Robert Pennells, a former employee who, by coincidence, was a second cousin to my friend, Kate Quarry. Kate's dad Allan was a great pal and a superb theatre organist with whom I shared a very special evening in St Paul's Cathedral whilst rehearsing for a recital, for which he was turning my pages. Allan always protested that he didn't read music, but he did a first-rate job. It was awesome to be alone in that extraordinary building and wander around, completely undisturbed, with just the stray amber glow from the external floodlights streaming through the cathedral's windows. Back to school ...

We also visited St Peter's Organ Works, the factory of N.P. Mander in Bethnal Green. Noel Mander's son John was also at CLS, although a couple of years ahead of me. His father would regularly loan a small chamber instrument to the school for performances of classical masses by the likes of Mozart and Haydn.

In my third year at CLS, I changed piano teachers to study with, at his own suggestion, Roy Wilkinson – lessons being after school. In truth, lessons with my teacher at the Guildhall had become somewhat unreliable and economical in length, and I suspect Cimbro Martin was

Allan Newman playing during my break in St Paul's Cathedral.

having personal difficulties. Whilst the new arrangement at school was less than comfortable at times (I think Roy had his own challenges), I probably made swifter progress than formerly. In retrospect, it was rather curious for someone to come up and say that they "would like to teach you" …

The musical traditions and opportunities at CLS were considerable. In my time there were two first-rate choirs, the main school choir and the 'special choir', and there was also an orchestra in which I was later to play the double bass. I also contributed to the percussion section, along with my friend Alan Wilson. I had to cope with the likes of the solo side drum rolls in Rossini's *Thieving Magpie* Overture as well as the xylophone part for Saint-Saëns *Danse Macabre*. As well as playing the organ, my long-standing school friend, Peter Bullett, would be playing in the cello section. Some staff members also supported the orchestra. There was a large-scale school concert each year, and for one of these, I remember playing the piano for a concert performance of Smetana's *The Bartered Bride*. In my last year, I was asked to play the Grieg Concerto (I seemed to spend much of my life playing this work, to the amusement of some), and in the second half, the choir sang Haydn's *Nelson Mass* with soprano April Cantelo.

I had an interesting experience in 1964 when the school volunteered me to be one of four drummer-boys to appear in Benjamin Britten's *Billy Budd* on stage at the Royal Opera House. We were so well drilled that I can still tap out the lengthy rhythm we had to play. I met Britten briefly in the wings of the stage on the last night before he took his bow.

Lunchtimes at school were frequently occupied with a choir rehearsal. At other times, some of us could be found in the Great Hall, either practising on the Chappell concert grand piano or the ageing and asthmatic organ upstairs. As Peter Bullett has poignantly reminded me, this was a potentially friction-filled time with the Chess Club, which met in the body of the hall and didn't always take kindly to additional stimulation from our musical offerings!

Instrumental teachers at school included many whom I didn't know at the time but who have become colleagues over the years, including the trumpeter William (Bill) Houghton and harpist Osian Ellis, with whom I shared meals regularly on tour with the London Symphony Orchestra.

End of first year at the City of London School • Class 02B • Form master Bernard 'Bunny' Ross (summer 1964)

The violin teacher was Renée Clare, whose husband, Edward Spratt, taught the trumpet. She was quite a force to be reckoned with, but she did allow our star violinist Adrian Levine to lead the orchestra. Adrian has gone on to be a greatly respected violinist as a member of the English Chamber Orchestra and leader of many other major orchestras as well as a professor at the Royal College of Music (RCM). A little ahead of him was the violinist Eugene Danks, who went on to play for the BBC Symphony and Royal Philharmonic orchestras. Before me at CLS was the organist Ian LeGrice, who acted as assistant organist at Temple Church whilst still at school, a position that was later formalised when Dr John Birch became organist and officially appointed Ian as assistant organist. Starting at CLS a year or two after I left was the famous cellist, Stephen Isserlis. One of my current orchestral pianist colleagues, Clive Williamson, was also at CLS, although somewhat after me. I spend much of my life playing the music from the Harry Potter films, and it's a little-known fact that Harry Potter also attended CLS, although quite how he juggled this with Hogwarts is beyond me.

The CLS choir and instrumentalists gave regular lunchtime recitals at city churches as well as schools further afield, such as St Paul's, Hammersmith, and Charterhouse in Surrey. There were two occasions each year that I particularly looked forward to, the first of these being the annual carol service. This was held in the school hall, and one of the physics teachers, Arthur (Archie) Campbell (a terrific pianist and also playing the organ, French horn and double bass), brought an electronic organ to school, which he had built and which he played for the occasion. From 1965, the service was held in Temple Church, a short walk from the school and also the organ seat of the famous Dr George Thalben-Ball. Choristers from this church received a scholarship to attend CLS, as did the Children (choristers) of the Chapel Royal. Like the Temple Church choristers, most of us were totally in awe of this legendary musician, affectionately referred to as the 'Doctor'. He was frequently to be seen pacing the aisles of his church during our rehearsals, possibly generating a degree of anxiety for our organist. GTB, as he was generally known, was a native of Australia and had the distinction of having given the first UK performance of Rachmaninov's notoriously difficult Third Piano Concerto. If you wanted to have organ lessons with him, he would expect you to play him two Chopin studies on the piano – no mean expectation!

The other significant occasion for me was the Commemoration of Benefactors Service in St Paul's Cathedral, which probably led to my great love of this building – its music and heritage. On the day of the service, the choir would walk in file from the school to the great cathedral by way of the narrow cobbled lanes behind Victoria Street, ultimately walking the length of the imposing nave, under the magnificently gilded dome, and into the choir stalls. It would be true to say that I became fairly obsessed with this organ as a schoolboy and would spend ages copying out details of its specification from books. I think I always had a completely unrealistic dream that one year I might get to play the voluntary at the close of the service but, of course, that never happened, and if a pupil had been invited, it certainly wouldn't have been me. Still – we can all dream! I had to wait until the mid-nineties to play the instrument and with the console in its new position in the south choir gallery. Previously it was hidden from view behind a small panel in the north choir organ case, and there was always great amusement when that panel was opened to facilitate a view of what was happening down in the choir, revealing the beaming face of Martin Roberts, who would be undertaking the organist's duties.

Martin joined the music staff in September 1965, following the departure of Dr John Wray (director of music) to be warden of the Royal Manchester College of Music (and principal from 1970 until the college's incorporation into the new Royal Northern College of Music), and Roy Wilkinson took over his position. Martin brought with him a remarkable array of qualifications for a first teaching job. He was only a few years older than some of the boys, and yet he had studied at the Royal Academy of Music (RAM), St John's College, Cambridge, and Magdalen College, Oxford – holding degrees from both London and Cambridge universities. Whilst at CLS, Martin also ran the naval section of the Combined Cadet Force (CCF) – he was held in great esteem and affection by his pupils.

Boys were required to participate in the CCF and we could choose which service to join. My father had been in the RAF when he was younger, although he was too young to see active service. I therefore thought I would follow in his footsteps, putting the navy second, although ,in the event, they put me in the army! We spent many 'happy' hours late on Monday afternoons learning to parade around the playground, disassemble and reassemble rifles, and stand still without moving, which I found as difficult then as I did years later when trying to stand still in the arena at a Prom. The CCF would go on camp to a military establishment in the area of Borough Green in Kent, and this was actually quite fun as we were allowed to go on 'night manoeuvres', which meant legally staying up late and trying not to get lost. We also went on the occasional visit to a firing range near St James's Park, and to my surprise, I found that I was able to hit a stationary target. The CCF was run by two NCOs who filled us with a degree of terror. They could be quite vindictive when the mood took them, and so we were always most particular about the level of shine on our boots when we left home on Monday mornings! For my last two years at CLS my form master was Dr Pat Whitmore. Apart from being head of French, he was also commanding officer for the CCF and, unknown to us at the time, he had helped to liberate French villages during World War II. Martin Roberts tells me that at Dr Whitmore's funeral, he was greeted by the mayor of one of those villages.

My father was passionate about sport and had played a great deal of rugby until his marriage, when Mum became concerned about the regularity of his broken bones and dislocated shoulders. I did not inherit his passion, although I had always enjoyed swimming. At CLS,

Wednesday afternoon was, unfortunately for me, sport – just sport, and this was not a good thing. I therefore have no idea how I allowed myself to be signed up to play rugby, a sport I had never played and didn't have any inclination to play. Even more unfortunate as most sports took place at the CLS sports ground in Grove Park, South London – a fair travelling distance and in the wrong direction for getting home. Somehow, I found the courage to salvage the situation in time and managed to change to swimming, which took place in the pool on the school's premises. This was a much more satisfactory arrangement and it also meant an earlier return home to deal with the little matters of homework, piano practice and building electronic circuits. I only ever went to Grove Park twice for the annual cross country race, and I have no idea how I survived that!

At this time, the school-leaving age was fifteen and most of us started at CLS in year two – the first year (age ten-eleven) being assigned to the Junior School at the far end of the playground. After four years, pupils sat 'O' levels and then entered the sixth form for two or three years. For the most part, life at CLS was extremely good – we had some remarkable teachers (masters), and I was very lucky with the musical opportunities that came my way, as well as the friendships made.

For reasons explained later, in late 1966, I formally sat an entrance audition for the Royal Academy of Music, the panel being the pianist Max Pirani and his specialist aural colleague, the legendary Eric Fenby (Delius's amanuensis). It would be fair to say that my decision to leave school in 1967 at the end of the fifth form (fourth year at CLS) to go and study at the RAM was not greeted with unbounded enthusiasm. In fact, it resulted in a summons to the headmaster's office (James Boyes) – in effect, to ask whether I knew what I was doing, although he was far too polite to actually say that! I was as sure as a fifteen-year-old lad could be – I knew I wanted to play the piano and this seemed the logical way forward.

Whether or not I made the right decision at that time is another matter. As life has panned out, I don't think I can say it was the wrong one, despite the seemingly idyllic attractions of university life. However, notwithstanding the expectations of my old school that I would stay on and take 'A' levels, I left the City of London School in July 1967 with eight 'O' levels and, no doubt, great hopes and expectations for the years ahead.

3 – The Redbridge Youth Orchestra

Late in 1965, I received a telephone call to say that a Redbridge Youth Orchestra (RYO) was being formed and asking whether I would like to play the Grieg Concerto in its inaugural concert – an invitation which was hugely exciting to a fourteen-year-old. The conductor was to be Charles Farncombe, primarily known for his association with the Handel Opera Society. The invitation came from the recently appointed music advisor for the new London Borough of Redbridge, Malcolm Bidgood OBE – an encounter that was to shape the rest of my musical life. Malcolm has an inexhaustible passion for music and musical education, and so far as the education committee was concerned, he was a force to be reckoned with when it came to supporting young musicians in the borough. In those early years, he provided me with countless opportunities to enhance my musical experience, not just with recitals and concertos, but also conducting the youth orchestra for numerous concerts. Like so many others from that golden period, I will forever owe Malcolm a huge debt of gratitude.

The year 1966 was a significant and life-changing one. A chance meeting between my father and Leslie England – a professor at the Royal Academy of Music, who had been a respected concert pianist – led to my having weekly lessons with him at the RAM. However my departure from the tutelage of my school's director of music was not without a certain acrimony, all the more so as my father had, ill-advisedly, chosen to explain this impending change to him during a social gathering following a concerto performance which he, his wife and Martin Roberts had attended. He was even less impressed when I decided to study full time at the RAM rather than Oxbridge, but I think you can only follow the path down which life seems to be leading you at the time.

In the mid- to late sixties, there was a group of enthusiastic staff and local players who met at William Torbitt School to play through orchestral repertoire in what was the infancy of the Redbridge Music School. On a few occasions I was invited to join them to play through part or all of a concerto, and this included Beethoven No. 1 (or No. 2) – in C. A pillar of the Music School was the lovely Joyce Reynolds, the secretary, who ran the organisation meticulously.

From the mid-sixties, I could often be found propping up a double bass – learning an orchestral instrument was Malcolm's suggestion, as he felt that a knowledge of an orchestral instrument would be a great asset. How right he was, and doing so also led to all sorts of playing experiences and fun

John Ridgeon and Joyce Reynolds, Aldeburgh (1968)

social possibilities. The instrumental options at the time in the Redbridge Music School had been the bassoon or the double bass but, due to availability, the double bass won the day, and I think that bassoon sections everywhere had a lucky escape. I had lessons with the veteran bass player Eric Halfpenny and was now able to join in the various activities of the local youth orchestra, not least the musical and non-musical delights of the yearly residential course in Aldeburgh and the end-of-course concert in the newly opened The Maltings concert hall at Snape.

Another of Malcolm's suggestions was that I teach the piano to his daughter, Vanessa. This I did for several years, driving to the Bidgood family home and enjoying the tea brought to me by Vanessa's lovely mum Daphne (who departed this life all too soon). At the end of the lesson, Malcolm and I would usually have quite a lengthy chat to put the world of music to rights.

Malcolm arranged a series of concerts called Soirée Musicale, which gave performance opportunities to those of us who wanted to take part. There was also a staff/student orchestra, Musici, which enabled more experienced students to join with staff for professional concerts.

Great friendships were forged in those early Aldeburgh courses, that still exist today. The orchestra would stay in two hotels on the sea-front – the White Lion and the Wentworth. Sectional rehearsals would be organised in the hotels as well as in the Jubilee Hall, which hosted the full orchestral rehearsals. Initially the course was under the guidance of conductor Charles Farncombe, and later, Ashley Lawrence, whom I was to encounter

Daphne and Vanessa Bidgood (c. 1970)

Redbridge Youth Orchestra playing at The Maltings, Snape • Rehearsal for Tchaikovsky Piano Concerto No. 1 (April 1969)

later in his role as principal conductor of the BBC Concert Orchestra (BBCCO). After-hours 'rehearsals' were arranged in members' hotel rooms, as frequently as they could be got away with!

Our first concert in The Maltings was in 1968, when the leader, Beverley Wood, played Tchaikovsky's Violin Concerto, and in the second half, the orchestra played Berlioz's *Symphony Fantastique*. The following year I was invited to play Tchaikovsky's First Piano Concerto in a concert that also included the premiere of the newly composed *Redbridge Variations* by Gordon Jacob. This had been commissioned as a tribute to the retiring chief education officer for Redbridge, Gilbert Miles, who had given music in our borough such remarkable support.

There was no piano in the Jubilee Hall, so we would trundle one down the High Street on loan from a possibly naive resident and to the great amusement of the locals. A piano was needed not only for the rehearsing of a concerto but also for the traditional Friday evening Informal Concert – an occasion we all very much looked forward to. This was an opportunity for orchestra members to let their hair down in front of an audience of

The great piano move • Malcolm Bidgood, Edward Garner, Howard Chilvers and leader, Tom Blackburn, Aldeburgh (April 1968)

mostly unsuspecting locals, who were treated to anything from Barbershop Quartets to renditions of Flanders and Swann, by way of Handel's *Water Music* for plastic duck and aleatoric radio effects, reminiscent of something from a *Doctor Who* soundtrack.

Cello coach Joan Bonner & Charles Farncombe (1968)

In those days, the hotels were rather more basic than today, so we always went prepared. The ability to stay in touch was crucial to our domestic survival, especially at night-time, so my chum Richard Tyler and I would take enough wire and telephone handsets to install the vital room-to-room communication system. We also prepared a rope ladder to allow easy passage in and out of the hotel after 'lights out'! Such activities may have been essential preparation for future orchestral touring.

These were great times – we gave fine performances of exciting and innovative repertoire to a very high standard, and the friendships from those days are treasured beyond measure. There were section tutors of great repute, including John Ridgeon, who was Redbridge's head of brass. John has developed a formidable worldwide reputation as an authority on the physical aspects of brass playing. Eventually, the decision was made to restrict the age range of orchestra members to school age. For better or worse, this decision immediately precluded the older and more experienced players who had already gone to study at music college or university. Of course, the orchestra continued to flourish, but not in quite the same way as previously and I know many of us felt disappointed that this, for us, was the end of an era.

Meanwhile, the Redbridge Youth Orchestra 'vets' still meet from time to time. In 2017 we returned to Aldeburgh to celebrate the orchestra's fiftieth anniversary as well as the ninetieth birthday year of Malcolm Bidgood. Almost a hundred members and guests sat down for a special meal, and we also managed a concert in our former rehearsal venue, the Jubilee Hall, with everyone joining together for a performance of

Glinka's overture *Ruslan and Ludmila* – conducted by luminary Bramwell Tovey. Several members had not picked up their instruments for more than thirty years and needed quite a bit of encouragement to do so. However, they eventually realised that the important aspect was taking part alongside others in that iconic building – one that, by good fortune, is next door to the Cross Keys pub. I lost count of how many people to whom I suggested that, should the going get tough, they simply mime – they don't encourage that at music college. Many have continued to play their instruments, inspired by the weekend. A large number has continued to play, as they did before that weekend, at the very highest levels of music-making in this country and abroad. Quite how I ended up organising that reunion in Aldeburgh remains something of a mystery. The initial approach from Malcolm to the Wentworth Hotel had elicited a highly enthusiastic response from the owner, Michael Pritt, who had remembered our visits from his father's time. Malcolm forwarded his reply to me with the words, 'over to you'!

In 2018, for Bram's first Radio 3 outside broadcast in his new role as principal conductor of the BBC Concert Orchestra (BBCCO), the orchestra's general manager Andrew Connolly and senior producer Neil Varley had agreed that a concert from our old stomping ground of Redbridge Town Hall would be an excellent idea. Neil, who is one of the most perceptive and tactful producers I've ever had the pleasure of working with, also suggested that a work by yours truly, being another native of Redbridge, would be very appropriate and so *Cygncopations* was programmed, with

Victoria Walpole playing the solo cor anglais part. The concert also included Gordon Jacob's *Redbridge Variations* and Britten's *Young Person's Guide to the Orchestra* (known in the trade as *YPG*). The concert was attended by a capacity audience that included a substantial number of RYO vets, many of whom had premiered the Jacob variations back in 1969 in The Maltings. We all met up after

With Bramwell Tovey and former RYO cellist Julia Vardigans (née Marshall), Luigi's restaurant, Gants Hill (2018)

Post-concert drinks in the Imperial College bar following Bram's Prom with the BBCCO ● Izzy Giles, Sue Eversden, Jennie Small, Bramwell Tovey, Clive Miller, Jane Miller, Ian Brown, Helen Fairmaner, Jonathan Venner, Ian Granger (August 2019)

the concert for a meal in Luigi's Italian restaurant at Gants Hill, where, fortunately, we had exclusive use of the main room, thus not causing too much mayhem to the other dinner guests.

A large group came to the Royal Albert Hall on the occasion of Bram's first Prom as principal conductor of the BBCCO, and I was delighted to be playing the organ for that concert. The 'vets' returned to Aldeburgh in 2020, again staying in the Wentworth Hotel – that great spirit of camaraderie ever-present. Although scheduled to propose the toast to absent friends, Bram was, unfortunately, unable to join us, so a video link was set up to 'fly him in' from Vancouver via cyberspace. As he wryly noted, this must have been the first occasion that an absent friend had proposed the toast to absent friends!

In addition to the occasional reunions, we also stay in touch through a dedicated Facebook page, and some of us meet up for significant birthdays. In 2019, many of us met to celebrate former RYO violinist Richard Tyler's seventieth birthday. This was broadly a recital of church and instrumental music – managing to rekindle our old habit of mixing our playing and conducting, whereby Richard conducted some items while I played and visa versa. Richard and his wife Sue's two talented sons, Dominic and Robin, also played the bassoon and cello.

Another founder member, Mary Spiers, who had previously celebrated her sixtieth in typically extravagant style with a performance of Holst's *The Planets* in Brentwood Cathedral, decided to celebrate her seventieth birthday in January 2016 with a *Last Night of the Proms* concert in the Brentwood Centre. I was privileged to contribute Grieg's Piano Concerto in which I managed a small twist – I incorporated the tune of 'Happy Birthday' at the climax of the cadenza, somewhat reminiscent of 'Roll out the Barrel' which Franz Reizenstein famously included at the

With Malcolm Bidgood, Brentwood (2016)

same moment in his *Concerto Popolare*, written for the 1956 Hoffnung Music Festival at the Royal Festival Hall. I may not get away with that again! Between ourselves – I was so frightened of forgetting the tune of 'Happy Birthday' at the crucial moment, I wrote it down and left it inside the piano. Following the performance, I was delighted to meet up with Malcolm Bidgood, who had come especially for the occasion. It was this meeting that led Malcolm to investigate a return to Aldeburgh. As can be seen from the photo, Malcolm has written his own fascinating book about the history of the Redbridge Music School.

Annual 'Informal Concert' in the Jubilee Hall, Aldeburgh (1969). Richard Tyler, Beverley Wood (hidden), Glinette Sim, Peter Dunkley, John Sibley, Russell Jordan, Paul Hart and Bramwell Tovey (l–r)

4 – In and Around Redbridge

In September 1970, I took up the position of organist at the United Reformed Church in Gants Hill, which had enthusiastic adult and young people's choirs. Here I was blessed with a wonderful assistant organist, Marion Perry, who was to go way beyond the call of duty in the years to come, routinely coping with last-minute-panic phone calls for her to play on a Sunday when work arose for me. The church also had a very good organ and a Steinway Model B piano (though sadly not both at the same pitch), so I frequently lost myself in the building for hours, practising for recitals and examinations.

Soon after my appointment, I decided that we should celebrate my first Christmas with a large-scale concert of choral and orchestral music, which would also give me an opportunity to try out my conducting 'skills'. Thinking back, I'm sure that the practicalities of setting this up caused substantial disorganisation and frustration to the smooth running of the church – pews and chairs went anywhere and everywhere, and on one occasion we rather thoughtlessly started to do this as the congregation was still leaving the church after the annual Service of Nine Lessons and Carols. However, the church members were very gracious about it, and we repeated the exercise for several years on the Sunday evening before Christmas. We went through some really exciting and varied repertoire, such as Elgar's *Enigma Variations*, although in retrospect, this was really too big a venture for a relatively small building. Still, we had fun! The organist on these occasions was always my friend Peter Bullett, who made regular visits to Gants Hill to join the musical festivities.

The church hosted Radio 2's *Sunday Half Hour* on one occasion, and the choir and congregation were also involved in an episode of *Songs of Praise* from St Andrew's Church, The Drive in 1976. For many years, my good friend Richard Tyler (and RYO violinist, who also lived in Ridgeway Gardens) was organist at the church opposite mine (St. George's) on the busy Woodford Avenue. Each year on Good Friday we would collaborate with a venture for the joint church choirs and orchestra. We would give a performance in one church and then launch the instruments over the busy dual carriageway outside and into the

Local choirs recording for a BBC Songs of Praise, St Andrew's Church, The Drive, Ilford (1976)

other. Eventually, common sense prevailed, and we simply gave one performance a year, alternating the venues.

Richard, myself and another good friend and RYO violinist, John Tombs, also developed a keen interest in amateur radio, sitting the City and Guilds Radio Amateurs Exam, which enabled us to get our transmitting license and pursue another hobby. John has since relocated to Tampa, Florida and I managed to meet up with him and his wife Glenda whilst on an orchestral tour in the late nineties – meeting old friends is one of the occasional and unexpected pleasures of orchestral touring.

For many years, John Roper, an RYO percussionist, was organist at St Laurence Church, Barkingside and we regularly joined for musical recitals there. In recent years, I understand that the organ and organist have become somewhat superfluous in favour of a more contemporary style of music-making – something I find very hard to be in sympathy with, being rather a traditionalist!

Many of us Redbridge-ites spent a good deal of time on Monday evenings commuting to the adjacent borough of Waltham Forest, which had a first-class professional/amateur orchestra called the Forest Philharmonic Orchestra, with many players being drawn from the local area, music colleges and the BBC Symphony Orchestra. The conductor at the time was Frank Shipway, a larger-than-life character and also a fine pianist (whom I saw give a stunning two-piano recital in Walthamstow with John Lill). He had been born in Birmingham and studied piano and percussion at the RCM. Despite being a person of grand gestures, he was a highly intuitive conductor, although he seemed to take some delight in creating awkward or embarrassing situations for those around him. On one occasion, he sat his elderly parents in front of the orchestra during a rehearsal and then proceeded to speak to a member of the woodwind section with a level of innuendo that made everyone cringe.

Frank achieved quite remarkable results through a combination of innate musicianship and creating a fear of humiliation. He had a unique musical persona, somewhat curiously modelled on Herbert von Karajan – for many years music director of the Berlin Philharmonic. Unfortunately, whilst this created a degree of amusement with the local orchestra, it hindered his wider progress to a substantial degree, as professionals wouldn't take him seriously. I always felt this to be a great loss to music-making in this country, as he was a significant musical talent and a fine orchestral accompanist for soloists. I remember watching him conduct (from memory) a performance of Rachmaninov's Third Piano Concerto with the pianist Shura Cherkassky, who took at least two wrong turns with optional cuts in the work. Frank was right there, guiding the orchestra without a hitch.

Some memorable performances with Frank were Elgar's *The Dream of Gerontius* at the Royal Festival Hall (1974), which was the first occasion that I played the organ in the hall. By chance, my dear friend from church, Marion Perry, was a friend of George Mann, the general manager of the hall, so I was able to arrange some private familiarisation time ahead of the concert day. The RFH instrument was designed by Ralph Downes – the celebrated organist, organ designer, RCM professor and for many years, organist at the Brompton Oratory. Downes had a particular concept in mind for this instrument, which he designed along classical lines. There is a wide divergence of opinion about this organ's suitability for larger-scale, orchestral and choral romantic repertoire – not least due to the instrument being a little underpowered when going into battle with such forces. I know that Downes was aware of this, although I don't

Sorry not to see you personally
For 1812, Generals ⑤ ⑥ ⑦
and ⑧ will give you all you
want (all played from Great). Good luck with Manfred!
[Pistons over solo manual]
                                If I might suggest it, be sure +
Kindly leave all boxes open!   use all 8 + 4 flue stops in the tutti.
Regards Ralph Downes.   Avoid "reeds alone" — it is too thin, on
                                this organ + sounds bad with orchestra.

                                Set up any pistons you want!

                                Hope to see you, Sunday am

                                        Ralph Downes

                                P.S. Have tuned as much as possible

                                        (of stop choir)
Just one thing I forgot — once the Positive /
organ has been tuned this evening, could
you kindly keep the motor (blower) OFF
until the beginning of the "Libera me"?
It doesn't do the organ any good for it
to be running continuously for hours without
playing!

        Ralph D.   I will drop in sometime towards the
                    end of your rehearsal, in case any problem
                    should arise — will you note it down if it
                    does, please

                    Thank you! Set any pistons you want + it's
        all yours. (Remember that the Full Organ, "red
        light" does not go off with the General Cancel; it
        is reversible, not moving the stops.
                            Good luck   Ralph Downes

A selection of notes left for me by Ralph Downes on the organ console in the Royal Festival Hall.

think that he ever publicly accepted there being an issue. The great man would regularly leave me a courteous note of greeting on the console or sometimes attend a rehearsal, walking up to the console at the end to say 'hello'. Following one rehearsal of *Belshazzar's Feast* with the LSO, he came along and anxiously asked, "Was that everything?" (meaning was I using all the stops).

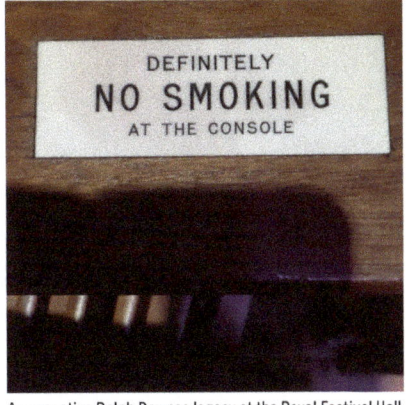

An evocative Ralph Downes legacy at the Royal Festival Hall.

He knew only too well that the organ should have the last say, coming in as it does to eclipse all the assembled forces. Unfortunately, without a little skulduggery, that's just not realistic.

On one occasion Downes came in at around 6:50pm as I was going through my set-up for that evening's performance of Mozart's Mass in C minor. The demands on a large organ for such a piece are relatively small, but he insisted on checking the tuning of one fairly loud stop (the Solo Harmonic Trumpet 8), which was not remotely in the equation for use in this performance. Unhappy with one note, he insisted on going inside the organ to tune it while I held down the offending note and the hall staff held the doors for ten minutes!

The organ's unenclosed design is stunning and a major visual impact in the hall. For a while this was under threat following the hall's refurbishment in 2005, when an appeal was launched, under the caring guidance of the organ's curator Dr William McVicker, to raise money to complete the organ's return to its rightful place. One lovely curiosity of a bygone age has been retained – the 'No Smoking' sign on the console!

In 1978, Forest Philharmonic and several massed choruses performed Mahler's monumental Symphony No. 8 (*Symphony of a Thousand*) at the Royal Albert Hall. Rehearsing at Queen Mary College in Mile End, I was poised to play the opening, solo full organ chord when I noticed that all the brass section had their instruments raised to play. Frank explained that he had written the organ part into the brass parts in case the organ in the RAH wasn't loud enough … those cue notes were never played!

Some other Forest Philharmonic Orchestra concerts that stick in the memory for other reasons are a performance of the *1812 Overture* in which Bramwell Tovey and I played the two obbligato bell parts, which was apparently a source of great amusement. The cannon part was performed on a bass drum with a microphone inside it, leading to inevitable issues with audio feedback in the concert and obvious displeasure from the maestro. In the concert programme, and with a typical sense of mischief, Frank had credited the cannon player as being the principal of Walthamstow College (where the orchestra rehearsed):

Principal Cannon

The Very Reverend Norman Lindop

The other memorable occasion, albeit seriously embarrassing for me, was a performance of Mozart's Requiem Mass, for which I was playing the organ part on a small Bontempi-style home entertainment organ – no doubt provided for a knock-down charge and with clearly no knowledge of what was required. After the rehearsal, some wag thought it would be fun to leave the instrument's rhythm box set to auto-start a bossa nova rhythm when I began to play – this was the first and fairly gentle entry of the *Kyrie* with the choir basses. I was in big trouble, and that was a life lesson – no matter how late you get back after a dinner break, always check the organ before you start the performance!

Others involved in those days will remember that a great highlight of each concert was the 'after-party', which was frequently held in Woodford at the home of Norman Thurston who played the viola and, at the time, administered the Aurelian Ensemble. They were also sometimes held in South Woodford at the home of the general administrator Gerald Rosen, a great supporter of the orchestra who had the novelty of a swimming pool at the end of his garden!

Frank made very few CDs, and those in this country were with the RPO. In 1996, he made a hugely respected recording of Mahler's Symphony No. 5 with them for the Tring label. This has subsequently been released by several different companies and remains one of the great recordings of this symphony. He died tragically in August 2014 at the age of seventy-nine, from injuries received in a car accident in Wedhampton, Wiltshire.

5 – The Royal Academy of Music and Beyond

Regressing to 1967, I embarked on six years' 'hard labour' at the Royal Academy of Music, supported again by Malcolm Bidgood and the Redbridge Education Committee. I encountered all the usual challenges of instrumental lessons in addition to harmony (Dr Arthur Pritchard), history of music (Dr Arthur Jacobs) and aural training (Dr Frederick Durrant) – there seemed to be a plethora of doctors and Arthurs during my student days. The aural classes could be rather scary, with such delights as sight-singing in C clefs (alto and tenor) in front of the class. My second study was a half-hour lesson on the double bass with, usually, John Walton, and sometimes Doris Greenish (whose father Arthur, I believe, wrote the standard tome on the rudiments of music).

My abiding memory of my first day at the RAM was all first-year students gathering in the main concert hall (the Duke's Hall) to be addressed by the principal Sir Thomas Armstrong who, with his wife Hester, lived in a flat to the rear of the Academy. Sir Thomas had a warm and kindly personality and was rather self-effacing about his own work – he had been organist at both Exeter Cathedral and Christ Church Cathedral, Oxford and was much respected. He composed all his life, mainly in the church and choir genres, and his immortal descant to 'O Little Town of Bethlehem' is still sung around the world every Christmas. A gentle and caring man, both he and his wife gave great support to the students. He would frequently be seen wandering around the building wearing a cardigan and carpet slippers, much to the amusement of the students. On this special occasion, he welcomed us and poignantly reminded us that we had likely come from a school or institution where we were the leading musical light. He cautioned us not to be downhearted when we realised that things might be a little different in our new place of study.

My other early memory of the RAM was the common room. Contrary to what might be perceived on stage, I've always been quite shy. Even now, I find it hard to walk into a social gathering of people I don't know – I've never felt comfortable edging into an established group of people. The old student common room was on the right as you walked down to the Duke's Hall and the pigeonholes from which you were expected to collect most RAM communications were thoughtfully at the far end. The room was set up rather like my GP's surgery, with chairs all around the outside, and I remember having to brace myself to walk its length, past the seated students who I perceived to be staring at me!

Whilst at the RAM, I was determined to try as many skills as possible. In addition to those already prescribed, I studied piano accompaniment (Rex Stevens), composition (Dr Arthur Pritchard) and conducting with Maurice Miles, sharing the course alongside a certain Simon Rattle. As part of this course, Maurice Miles rather expected that we would travel each week for an evening class that he ran in west London. Living at that time in Essex, I fear that I wasn't a regular supporter of this 'unique opportunity' and was clearly out of favour for my lack of support.

I experienced my first Radio 3 recording session whilst at the RAM, when Dr Pritchard asked if I would turn his pages for the recording of an organ recital at St John's Wood Church, where he was organist. I was excited at this opportunity to witness such a recording at first hand. I left home early to be sure I wasn't late – unfortunately, I had completely the wrong impression of which church this was and spent some time futilely banging on the door of a building close to St John's Wood station rather than opposite Lord's Cricket Ground! This was before the days of satnavs, of course, but remedied in good time by a phone call to Mrs Pritchard and an unwelcome run. Dr Pritchard also played for the University of London graduation ceremonies, which took place in the Royal Albert Hall. Resplendent in his doctoral robes, he would play beforehand and at select moments during the occasion. I was thrilled to again be asked to turn his pages – my first experience of standing close to that legendary organ, which was to become such a big part of my life in later years.

Many other musicians from Redbridge were contemporaries or just after me at the RAM, and these included the cellists Ann Baker, Cathy Giles, Hilary Jones, Janet Roberts, Jean Wilkens; violinists Alison Kelly, Jackie Shave and Kathy Shave; double bassist Christopher Freeman; pianist Margaret Boultwood; conductor, tuba player and pianist Bramwell Tovey; oboist and organist Jonathan Venner; organist and percussionist John Roper; and percussionist and composer Ian Hughes. Several at the time went to 'the other place' (RCM) – Joanne Boddington,

John Chimes, Judith Huggins, Gary Kettel, Martin Koch, Russell Jordan, David Silkoff and Jonathan Small. Meanwhile, Lisa Beznosiuk, Colin Paris, Christopher Stearn and Jennifer Thurston were at the Guildhall School of Music and Drama whilst violinists Elisabeth Perry and Krysia Osostowicz were studying at the Yehudi Menuhin School in Surrey. Apologies for any omissions or errors.

An experience midway through my studentship was to reshape my future musical life. A student conductor asked me to play the piano part for Kodály's *Háry János* suite (this famously opens with a big orchestral sneeze). The *Viennese Musical Clock* movement features a charming celeste solo – more about that instrument later. Perhaps anticipating the life to come, I also noted that this piece requires two keyboard players, making it quite 'good for business'! Although I had played the occasional keyboard part in local orchestras, this musical experience was a revelation, and I knew then that playing in orchestras, with its sense of community music-making and camaraderie, was what I wanted to do. However, I had absolutely no idea how to go about it – such advice was hard to come by at music colleges in those days.

Whilst at the RAM I survived a performance of Liszt's First Piano Concerto, during which one of the percussionists managed to fall asleep and therefore didn't play the famous triangle solos in the third movement (for that reason, the piece is frequently nicknamed the *Triangle Concerto*). Eventually, the conductor, Maurice Handford, by now incandescent with rage and disbelief, had found a coin in his pocket and was insistently tapping out the rhythm on the metal rail of the rostrum. I was actually very lucky that my concerto had been included. The original programme was to be just Mahler's Seventh Symphony – quite long in its own right but to which was added the overture *Ruslan and Ludmila* to facilitate the addition of the Liszt. I had prepared for this performance with Leslie England, who had always been an understandably demanding teacher. I remember him walking into the Duke's Hall at around 6:30pm, while I was nagging away at the memory of some passages in the concerto, and he simply said, not unkindly, "If you don't know it now, you never will!"

Leslie England, Ridgeway Gardens, Ilford (late '60s)

During my first nearly four years at the RAM, Leslie England and I worked through a Chopin study every couple of weeks, Mozart and Beethoven sonatas, many of Chopin's major works and numerous concertos, including Grieg, Liszt E flat, Tchaikovsky B flat and Schubert-Liszt *Wanderer Fantasy*.

It was with Leslie England that I first experienced perfect pitch at first hand – the ability to hear a musical pitch and say what note it is. His party piece was to stand at the far end of the piano and ask you to play a selection of random notes from one end of the piano to the other – around ten or so. He would then tell you the note names in the order you played them. He would do the same if you played a cluster of notes all at the same time. I remember this making me feel seriously inadequate until I appreciated that this was a gift that not many people possess. I find that I can usually identify certain keys, such as D flat and B flat, although I'm sure that for me, this is more a question of memory.

Since leaving school, I had always wanted to learn the organ properly. Apart from a natural attraction, I had a feeling that it would be useful for the future – how accurate that instinct was. Unfortunately, Leslie England had been emphatic that learning the organ would ruin my piano technique, so the idea had to be put on hold. By now, I had access to the local church (where I would become organist in 1970), so I could at least continue with the covert DIY organ tuition which had started at school.

Sadly, in my fourth year, Leslie England was taken ill, and I was passed around one or two other professors. Eventually, Christopher Regan (then director of studies) coaxed Vivian Langrish, the legendary member of the piano faculty, out of retirement to come in once a week to teach me – I felt truly honoured. He was the most extraordinary musician who simply oozed enthusiasm for everything we worked on together. Referring to an upcoming performance, he would ask, "So when does this balloon go up?" Significantly, he was the first teacher to finally convince me of the value of slow, firm practice. He also opened my ears to the power of harmony and would regularly play harmonically rich passages from symphonies or operas to prove his point. The Prelude to Wagner's *Tristan and Isolde* and the *Magic Fire Music* from *Die Walküre* come to mind. I would regularly visit his home in Beckenham, Kent for extra lessons with which he was immensely generous. Viv lived there with his wife, Ruth Harte, who was also a piano professor at the RAM as well as an international examiner for the ABRSM. His eightieth birthday was celebrated in style with a concert in the Duke's Hall of the RAM in 1974. This included Mozart's Concerto for Two Pianos with his long-term friend and duo partner, Egerton (Bob) Tidmarsh, for whom I turned pages – Ruth turned for her husband.

The Langrish's generously proportioned music room contained two full-size Bechstein grands and enough room for an audience of fellow students. This was the scene for numerous pupil recitals, which I admit to finding rather challenging. I will forever be grateful for the support and kindness shown to me by Viv and Ruth. More recently it has been good to feel a connection with them through their son Ian – a former pupil at CLS and a chorister under George Thalben-Ball at Temple Church.

Vivian Langrish didn't have a problem with my learning the organ, and Christopher Regan kindly arranged for me to have lessons with Douglas Hawkridge which, for the most part, took place in St. James' Church, Sussex Gardens, where he was organist. Douglas was a wonderfully pragmatic musician and teacher who knew exactly how to proceed with a self-taught organist having a long-term ambition to take an FRCO (Fellow of the Royal College of Organists) exam. He instilled a sense of discipline that carried me through the exam and into my later career.

During the early seventies, there was a good deal of music-making in Redbridge and this included the formation of a (broadly) student orchestra called Concerti Allegri – conducted by Bramwell Tovey. We gave some terrific concerts with a wide breadth of demanding repertoire and aways a great

Ruth Harte & Vivian Langrish's 80th, RAM (1984)

sense of fun, as per the group's name (cheerful/joyful concerts). There was also a Concerti Allegri chorus which I directed, and there was an interesting occasion when we took a (mostly) choral concert to the good people of Theydon Bois. The programme included Holst's somewhat obscure *Two Psalm Settings* and also the Tuba Concerto by Vaughan Williams which was played by Bram with me conducting. However, memories of that evening are rather superseded by events which took place on the way home. We were driving along the road from Theydon Bois to Abridge when we noticed a sheet of water moving stealthily across the fields, heading for the cars trying to leave Theydon – the River Roding had burst its banks. I remember this being something of a mind-focusing moment and concluding that there wasn't much to be done. All the cars were moving to the left of the road to stop, with the occupants getting out to maximise height, just in case. I had two performers in the car with me, Jennifer Thurston and Maxine Cohen, and they promptly removed their long skirts to avoid them getting soaked. I'm told that I removed my trousers, but I think that's probably a scurrilous rumour! The water rose inexorably through the floor of the car and we eventually abandoned ship for a while until the level dropped far enough to allow the car to start – a somewhat ignominious end to an otherwise delightful evening.

On another occasion when I was conducting a concert with Concerti Allegri, the programme (mostly choral) included Elgar's *Enigma Variations*, and on that occasion, Bram was sitting behind the orchestra playing the organ. The next time that he and I performed this work together was for his first broadcast concert on Radio 3 as principal conductor of the BBCCO, and he took great delight in recounting the story, thereby noting that now I was at the back playing the organ and he was on the podium – exactly as it should be!

Although a brilliant tuba player and pianist, and blessed with wonderful gifts of communication, Bram was always destined to conduct. After several years in the UK with various ballet companies, he settled in Canada as music director of the Winnipeg Symphony Orchestra where, in 1998, I had the great pleasure of joining him for some solo performances, as well as two fine performances of Mahler's Eighth Symphony. For this I had acted as repetiteur in chorus rehearsals to maintain a sense of fair play between the pianists of the various choirs taking part. After a tenure of twelve years, Bram eventually moved to be music director of the Vancouver Symphony Orchestra where he stayed for eighteen years until 2018. Prior to his appointment in Vancouver, I was somewhat amused to receive a call from the orchestra to, in effect, ask me for a reference!

With Concerti Allegri had come further opportunities for concerto experience. Of particular note was an evening in July 1974 in Redbridge Town Hall. The programme was Stravinsky's Wind Octet, Rachmaninov's Second Piano Concerto (for which I played the piano) and Holst's *The Planets*. It's interesting to remember that Simon Rattle (who at the time was dating our principal cellist Cathy Giles and whom we saw quite frequently) came and played the prominent celeste part superbly on the glockenspiel (he did later move to the piano for *Neptune*, conceding defeat with its rapid scales and arpeggios, which would be impractical on the glock). Meanwhile, I was offstage conducting the ethereal and notoriously challenging ladies' chorus, and playing the organ part when necessary.

As an aside, there have been many memorable performances of *The Planets* over the years, though not all memorable for the best of reasons, usually associated with the magical but demanding choral ending which is ultimately sung 'a cappella' (unaccompanied) by two groups of ladies' voices, each with several vocal parts. An additional complication is that the singers are frequently positioned at some distance from the stage and with no real pitch or rhythmic references. One such occasion was at the Royal Festival Hall when the offstage ladies had been positioned behind the choir doors and, as frequently happens, the choir went flat. At the end of the rehearsal, the choir mistress popped her head enthusiastically round the choir door to ask if all was well. The conductor, Matthias Bamert, brought the house down with, somewhat atypically, "Yes – it is just that the orchestra is a little sharp!"

When younger, I did a fair bit of conducting, even deputising for Bram on one occasion, for ballet performances at Sadler's Wells! However, for the most part, my efforts were concentrated on the choral side of music, and for a while, I was an occasional guest chorusmaster for the Royal Choral Society, preparing them for a performance and recording of Handel's *Messiah*. This was actually a very interesting experience, and it had been agreed with the conductor, Owain Arwel Hughes, that we would try to achieve some more authentic tempi than had become traditional in this country. In principle, this meant things going rather more briskly than everyone was accustomed to!

In the summer of 1973, I spent a couple of weeks in the south of France with Jennifer Thurston, who was a violin pupil of Yfrah Neaman at the GSMD. I think he offered a degree of pressure to attend the summer school there, for which he was a violin tutor. No doubt a similar type of encouragement to that which I had experienced from Maurice Miles to sign up for his conducting evening classes in Chiswick during my time on the RAM conducting course! We stayed in Nice midst sweltering summer temperatures (something I've always found challenging) and most days we would make the long climb to the course centre, which was in the hills behind the town. Also on this course was my good friend Geoffry Wharton, an American violinist whom I had met several times in London, both for lessons with maestro Neaman at the GSMD as well as at student parties. He had also played solo violin in concerts with Concerti Allegri. Geoffry spent most of his professional life as associate concertmaster of the Cologne Philharmonic Orchestra.

At the time of the course in Nice, we had been working on the César Franck Sonata for Violin and Piano. We both shared a slightly wacky sense of humour and were prone to ad-libs and moments of jazz improvisation whilst rehearsing. A leading French classical radio station had been in Nice for a feature on the course and one morning we were asked whether we would play them the second movement of the Franck – the hard one! They asked for a balance test, so off we went. We must have had a sixth sense about exactly what they were up to, as we played from the start and kept going, despite being under the impression that this was a balance rehearsal and we would be stopped. We reached the end and went out to the engineers to ask whether we could hear something from their test. *"Non!"* was the curt reply – it had apparently gone out live. We could have been in so much trouble ...

Some of our student grant in those days was spent in the Nightingale – our pub of choice in Wanstead and a regular Friday-night haunt for the local 'musos'. An occasional visitor on those occasions was Mike Hatch, who was set to become one of the world's leading recording engineers, and with whom I've worked on many occasions.

I left the RAM that summer with a raft of exciting and potentially useful skills under my belt. However, as I was to discover, in those days they didn't teach us some of the finer points of orchestral life, such as how to set about getting to work during transport strikes, what to do if your bow-tie fastening breaks, what to do if a waiter spills curry sauce down the front of your dress shirt (the answer to that is later on) or how to get from a recording session in London to one in Watford when your schedule is changed at the last minute and you only have forty-five minutes to get there. The solution to that came from the RPO's orchestra manager, Sally Sparrow, booking me a Virgin bike for a white-knuckle ride along the Finchley Road and up the M1. Somewhat unhelpfully, I was not allowed to put my arms around the rider and remember sitting there with the speedo nudging seventy and, frighteningly, leaning backwards to enable me to reach the handles behind! I was sitting on the soloist's stool with five minutes to spare but in no fit state to play for rather longer (Spolianski film music piano features with the BBC Concert Orchestra and Rumon Gamba, 2008). Such film concertos have become a big part of my musical life, both in recording and performance.

White-knuckle ride from Sloane Square to Watford Colosseum (2008)

6 – The Redbridge Youth Choir

In the years immediately after leaving the RAM, I managed to keep the wolf from the door by teaching, both privately and for the local authority. I also helped to set up the Redbridge Youth Choir (RYC) alongside soprano, Ruth Saye (who taught singing in Redbridge) and also 'he who shall not be named' – he only lasted a couple of terms, as he didn't like power-sharing. This choir complemented a girls' choir which was directed by Edna Graham, a member of the music school staff but formerly a respected coloratura soprano who had performed at Covent Garden and other major venues. The choir gave some terrific concerts, including memorable performances (with orchestra) of the Brahms, Fauré and Mozart Requiem settings together with Vivaldi's setting of the Gloria, Haydn's *Nelson Mass* and many smaller works. The choir made a superb Christmas LP in 1980 called *Christmas Gift*. This recording was made in St Alban's Church, Holborn – a building with a fine acoustic and a very loud organ! We recorded with the choir upstairs in the gallery, and I directed from the organ console.

I actually knew this organ very well, as I had played it many times for Sunday services, especially during the organist's interregnum and

The soprano section recording Christmas Gift (April 1980)

Choir view of mission control.

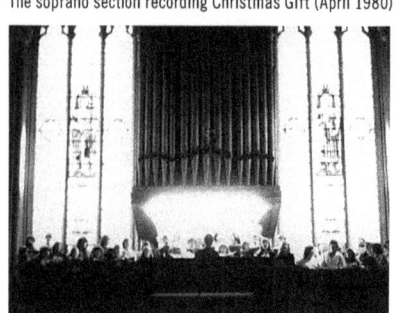
Up, up and away in St. Alban's Church, Holborn.

Trumpets (and trombones) from the Redbridge Youth Orchestra.

also when the services included Venetian Masses with the professional choir and a small orchestra. For most of that period the choir was directed by Ronald Corp, now a well-known conductor and composer, and formerly, librarian to the BBC Singers and Symphony Chorus. We have worked together more recently on a number of recording projects with the BBCCO for Mike Dutton's highly respected Epoch CD label. Ron and I had actually met some years earlier for concerts, as he had studied at Christ Church College, Oxford alongside another good friend from CLS, Stephen Fielding. Whilst at school, Stephen had been in the choir of Her Majesty's Chapel Royal, which had a similar arrangement with CLS as Temple Church. Ron, Stephen and I gave numerous recitals together in Stephen's church in Potters Bar. They both sang (unlike me), and Stephen was also a highly accomplished pianist and organist. I remember us periodically searching for *The Lost Chord* or inviting Maud into the garden!

Eventually, Michael Fleming, warden of the Royal School of Church Music, became the new organist at St Alban's and my visits became far less frequent. The church has a very 'High' tradition and used to pride itself on being higher than Rome. On at least one occasion I remember setting off up the stairs to the organ loft and the incumbent priest (the aptly named Peter Priest) calling after me, "I think it's going to be a good show today!" Whilst carrying out research for my album of organ music by Percy Whitlock, I was delighted to discover that Peter Priest was the dedicatee of the Divertimento from the Four Extemporizations for Organ. I digress …

In the summer, the Redbridge Youth Choir would spend a week at the London Borough of Redbridge's outdoor pursuits centre, Glasbury House, located in Glasbury-on-Wye, just along the river from that great town of books, Hay-on-Wye. A fantastic team-building exercise, which cemented relationships which last to this day. We specialised in any activity that could in some way be classified as moderately dangerous, such as abseiling, climbing mountains, caving, walking through river gorges, around narrow mountain passes and underground passages, riding horses (and falling off them) and raft-building. We would also make regular night-time walks to see how many people we could get into the local telephone box, and this became something of a tradition. I think the

Still trying, twenty years on ...

record was thirteen, although rather fewer when we've tried it during more recent 'grown-up' visits. Sometimes, more formal night-time activities were mounted, such as an interesting type of nocturnal hide-and-seek, which could lead to unexpected and fun encounters due to the lack of light.

The choir also made a particular study of escaping dormitories after 'lights out' for miscellaneous nefarious activities, all the while trying not to alert the staff. The 'long-suffering' staff had meanwhile been attempting to intercept such attempts, by methods that included us setting up thin string tripwires across the dormitory doorways (with keys attached), whilst simultaneously negotiating special treats from the young choir members such as 'apple-pie' beds! It was very good-natured, though I have no idea how anyone managed to get any sleep.

This continued until the early eighties. However, in 1995 we decided to make a return visit to Glasbury House, staying, in those days, in the Bunkhouse, a separate and self-contained building closer to the river. Initially, this just had one large dormitory sleeping sixteen and offering opportunities for much night-time amusement. We also had our own kitchen and a BBQ, so most basic needs and creature comforts were met.

It was good to be back, and even if age had taken its toll on our physicality it was reassuring to know that our minds didn't seem to have matured unduly! The RYC vets still make that annual visit, as well as meeting up for meals and a yearly BBQ. At the time of writing, they still paddle kayaks from Glasbury to Hay (and generally don't fall in). However, the abseiling, climbing, caving and other more strenuous activities have rather lapsed. I particularly enjoyed caving – the potential challenge of claustrophobia and that special silence of an underground cavern.

Over the years the establishment progressively 'sanitised' the Bunkhouse to the point that it was so modernised, with stainless steel fittings and washable, epoxy flooring, that it lost most of its charm. They even covered up the charming and very old wooden fireplace, which we believe was inscribed 1854. In 2015, Redbridge Council made the (to my mind) short-sighted decision to sell the house – what a loss to countless Redbridge schoolchildren, who would gain so much from visiting. We were the last guests there, and since then we have stayed in Tylau Lodge, closer to Hay. Glasbury is always in our hearts, though, and the base for our kayaking and telephone-box hunting – our old box was removed some years ago.

And so, it came to pass that back in April 1977 I found myself sitting in the lounge of the Wentworth Hotel in Aldeburgh talking to William Relton, at that time the general manager of the BBC Symphony Orchestra. On this occasion he was wearing the hat of conductor for the Redbridge Youth Orchestra's Easter course, for which I had prepared the Redbridge Youth Choir for a performance of Elgar's *From the Bavarian Highlands*. He asked me about myself, and I told him what I would like to be doing. He enquired whether I had written to his orchestra and, by chance, it was the one orchestra that had not replied – he was embarrassed to hear that and the conversation may have proved, unwittingly, to have changed the path of my career.

Another great collaboration between the Redbridge Youth Orchestra and Choir was for a performance of Holst's *Hymn of Jesus.* This was something of a borough-wide venture involving not just the Youth Choir but also other Redbridge Music School choirs, together with staff from some of the borough's schools and music service. Although I was acting as chorus master, due to the indisposition of the scheduled conductor, I also conducted the performance in The Maltings, Snape (1981). The *Hymn of Jesus* is an extraordinary piece of music, greatly influenced by oriental instruments and techniques, that are very powerful alongside the highly challenging orchestral writing and divisi choruses. Despite this, the work is very rewarding to perform and listen to. At one point in the final rehearsal, I turned round to see whether a

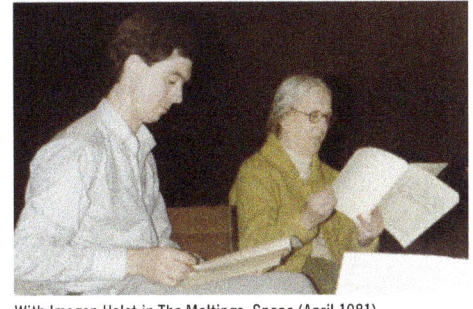

With Imogen Holst in The Maltings, Snape (April 1981)

colleague in the hall could advise on balance. Somewhat unexpectedly, I saw the unmistakable figure of Imogen Holst sitting there – someone who had always been very welcoming to the orchestra in Aldeburgh. This was quite a challenging realisation! I went down to ask whether she would like to come and meet the assembled company. She was very gracious and sat on the rostrum for quite some time, enthralling us with details of the work, its influences and how it came to be written. What a treat and what a day we had – the orchestra and choir gave their all and everyone rose to the occasion. As always, I had been hugely supported by the enthusiasm and vocal expertise of my co-director, Ruth Saye.

Along the way, the Redbridge Youth Choir was responsible for the yearly January pantomimes, which included *Aladdin, Cinderella, Dick Whittington* and *Babes in the Wood*. I remember putting on some tights for one of them – likely *Dick Whittington*! We had great fun, and the hilarious scripts for these occasions were always written by the borough's percussion teacher and RYO's percussion coach, George Lawrence. Another major production was John Gay's *The Beggar's Opera,* which was supported by a small group of instrumentalists drawn from the Redbridge Music Service. This was produced, as were a number of operas in the borough, by Hilary Liddell, a noted actress who was married to the actor Bernard Hepton. Her sister Nona Liddell was a highly respected violinist.

As with the Redbridge Youth Orchestra, the Redbridge Youth Choir forged lifelong friendships, assisted greatly by the yearly visits to Glasbury. For many, it has also developed a long-term love of choral singing, with many members still singing in choirs around the country.

Harem scene from *Cinderella* with the Redbridge Youth Choir (1979)

An early attempt at capsizing (1977)

Co-director Ruth Saye at the RYC barn dance (1977)

Raft construction (1979)

After hours planning (1982)

Porth yr Ogof cave. Seriously? Down there? (late '90s)

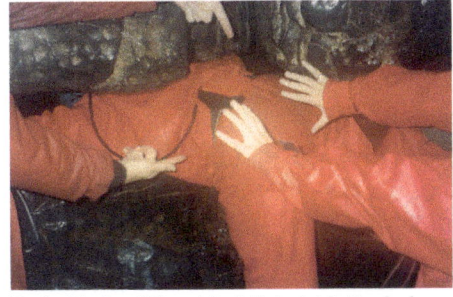

'Posting' Tim Everett through the 'letterbox' at Porth yr Ogof.

Sky Trek Challenge at Llangorse (August 2010)

Jo and Matthew kayaking from Glasbury to Hay (2019)

7 – The BBC

In an ongoing attempt to work out how to achieve my ambition of spending time as an orchestral keyboard player, I had been writing letters to the orchestra managers of the country's symphony orchestras. Although I'm quite ambitious, it's not in my nature to be pushy and hassle people for work, and I would never want to tread on other people's toes. I also attended rehearsals when invited by friends, courteously introducing myself to other keyboard players, of whom I was in awe, of course. In this profession, as in most walks of life, there's a natural order of things: there is already an established list of players who have reasonable expectations of work coming their way!

I received a string of replies to my letters thanking me for writing, explaining how things work, and saying they would keep my name on file. Today there seems to be something of an air of entitlement from some of the younger generation that, together with a particularly sycophantic use of social media, I personally don't find endearing. Luckily, most orchestra managers are not that fickle and can see through this behaviour, but not all. Good things come to those who wait – you just need to be known and known to be reliable, pleasant and proficient.

Late in 1977, and a few months after my chat with William Relton in Aldeburgh, I was booked by the BBCSO for a pre-recorded studio concert due to take place in March the following year. I always considered that to be my first 'proper' professional engagement, at least in terms of being engaged by an established orchestra, and that call was something of a watershed. I have no recollection of the repertoire, but I know that one piece involved two keyboard players. This was the first occasion that I met my good friend Malcolm Hicks, for many years organist to the BBCSO and always seen at the 'mighty beast' in the RAH for the Last Night of the Proms. As I recall, I was playing the harpsichord and Malcolm was playing the piano. I remember being acutely aware of the microphones and, with them, the awareness that this performance would not only be shared with the audience in the hall but also with a large radio audience. That feeling remained with me for some considerable time, but eventually the technology became part of the furniture, to my great relief.

What made this concert particularly satisfying was that it was broadcast from the Duke's Hall of the Royal Academy of Music, and part of my role was to hit the strings inside the treasured Steinway concert grand with timpani sticks – each to his own, I guess. Doing anything inside this piano would have been a serious crime a few years earlier as a student, and here we were in full view of the principal, Sir Anthony Lewis, and many members of the professorial staff, sitting in the balcony beaming down on us! For the most part, this sort of activity, along with other similar acts of violence towards pianos, is more usually carried out during the recording of film soundtracks. Indeed, much of my work on the films *Aliens* and the *Lord of the Rings* trilogy involved just that, either with percussion beaters or metal bars. Quite reasonably, most hire firms reserve special (or not-so-special) pianos to receive such gestures of affection.

This concert at the RAM led almost immediately to further engagements with the BBCSO. I was lucky that there had apparently been recent changes to their 'extra' list – the ordered list of players who would be engaged. These engagements included my first foreign tour – to Eastern Europe. Three weeks starting in Vienna and ending in Paris, and taking in several countries that were, at the time, still behind the Iron Curtain. The repertoire included Stravinsky's complete *The Firebird* ballet and Bartók's *Music for Strings, Percussion and Celesta* with conductors Pierre Boulez and Sir Charles Mackerras. Interestingly, although Pierre Boulez travelled on the coach with the orchestra, Mr Mackerras travelled in a limousine – this situation reminded me of André Previn's first trip to the USA with the London Symphony Orchestra, when I understand he spurned the limo to travel by coach, wanting to know what the travelling was like for the members of his orchestra.

Originally for this tour, I was engaged to play the prominent piano part in the Bartók, as the personnel manager (fixer) assumed that the celeste, being the named instrument in the work's title, was the major part – big mistake! I had already spent an intensive and somewhat panicky couple of weeks learning the piano part before the orchestra rang to say that there had been a mistake and the other player would be playing the piano. I think 'the other player' had wondered who this youngster was who was suddenly leaping in to play the solo part! This was Richard Nunn

– an interesting character and a fabulous repetiteur who had been on the staff at the Royal Opera House, Covent Garden and the Royal College of Music, and who had an expert knowledge of opera. He was very good to me in my early days, although he later took against me when he lost favour with some orchestras and assumed, quite incorrectly, that I had somehow blackened his name – very sad. Freelancers don't have that sort of power. You just do your best to keep your head down and do your job as well as possible, not complaining or telling tales about other players.

Later in 1978, I joined the BBCSO for my first Prom. The Proms is usually regarded as the largest music festival in the world, and it's always exciting to play in one of the concerts. This particular concert was quite a novel introduction, as we were playing Lutosławki's *Mi-parti* with conductor James Loughran – this is not the most traditional musical language, although a very effective piece of music. At that time, the stage walk-ons (bull runs) were each side of centre stage, with a short backstage corridor between them. For some reason, one of the doors had been left open, and a couple of the Royal Albert Hall's staff were walking past. Clearly hearing what we were up to, and not understanding it, one asked of the other, in a very loud voice, "What the f***k's that?" The effect on the orchestra was quite dramatic as this resounded around the hall!

A somewhat comical situation arose with the BBCSO when we were due to record a programme of music written and conducted by the American composer Gunther Schuller. The orchestral parts were appallingly presented, and most of them were cut-down versions of the full score. As I remember, there was a keyboard section of four players with its own score bearing just the four pairs of staves for our instruments. However, during the binding process, the instrument names had been cut off. This in itself might not have been a problem if the instruments had remained in the same order from page to page. Unfortunately, as in my case, I would be playing the keyed-glockenspiel part on the top system of a page, turn over and discover that the notes I was playing on the top system were now, in fact, the celeste part – these errors extended to other sections. We tried valiantly, but it was a non-starter. The maestro's suggestion that we all stay in the studio at lunchtime to copy out our own parts was not particularly well received, and the recordings were summarily cancelled.

I joined the orchestra for several of their regular Radio 3 Wednesday concerts at the Royal Festival Hall, and I always felt sad that the audience numbers were so low. As my friends will know, I have never really appreciated concerts of more adventurous contemporary music, which I simply don't understand. However, whilst many BBCSO concerts would contain more avant-garde repertoire, not all did, and it was a shame that such extensive preparation and effort was not better rewarded.

One Wednesday, we were in the RFH to rehearse Schoenberg's *Jacob's Ladder,* which had several offstage choirs and instrumental groups – one of these involved me. These groups were relying on CCTV in order to see the conductor, Christoph von Dohnányi (grandson of the pianist and composer Ernst von Dohnányi). The offstage television support was not working, and the maestro was getting impatient as we couldn't start the rehearsal. Eventually, a brave member of staff went onstage to reassure him that they were working on the problem. "Don't verk on zee problem, verk on zee solution," he barked!

One of the very happy traditions to have arisen from those days with the BBCSO was the annual Christmas keyboard meal. At first this involved Malcolm Hicks, Harold Lester, Richard Nunn and myself, but we were later joined by John Alley – all very BBC orientated. After some years the circle expanded to include players working with other symphony orchestras, such as Leslie Pearson, Vivian Troon, Michael Round, Michael Hyatt, Martin Goldstein, Elizabeth Burley, Alistair Young, Shelagh Sutherland, Clive Williamson, Bernard Robertson, Helen Crayford and Lindsay Bridgewater. Others have joined over the years, and numbers have ranged from half-a-dozen to twenty or so. Initially, this occasion was before Christmas and based in the Maida Vale area, but for many years now we have been located more centrally in London's Chinatown – currently Imperial China in Lisle Street – meeting early in the New Year. In practice, this is now more a meeting of friends with a history of working together over many years, together with their partners.

Work with the BBCSO led to an introduction to the BBC Concert Orchestra (BBCCO), which I joined for the first of many recordings of the Radio 2 programme *Melodies for You*, playing *Dance of the Sugar Plum Fairy* (on celeste). For those who don't know, the celeste is a small, piano-like keyboard instrument that, when moved, makes a sound somewhat reminiscent of an aircraft drinks trolley, though sadly without the same benefits. Until the arrival of Mr Potter and his owl, this was the archetypal celeste solo and one that has probably led to more interpersonal debate with conductors than any other piece. One extremely rude player/conductor took me to task one day for playing the cadenza 'out of time'. Now, if this piece is taken too fast then it frequently becomes musically necessary, as on this occasion, to take a bit of time in the celeste's free cadenza passage, otherwise it can sound like a manic scramble. Unfortunately, this gentleman was struggling to follow this straightforward passage and barked at me across the orchestra,

"How do you expect the dancers to dance if you don't play in time?"

Now, I'm not usually one to make a fuss, but I did rather take exception to this. After all, we're all entitled to a little natural courtesy. Maybe a trifle ill-advised but being so incensed at his rudeness, I pointed out to him that the dancers don't actually dance at that point. "Just play in time," was the reply! During the break, I saw him approaching ... here we go, I thought – but nice as pie he said, "You don't mind playing in time do you; otherwise I can't follow?" I said that we had realised this and that I would do my best for him. I hate confrontation, but there are limits beyond which I feel you need to stand up for yourself! The same gentleman clearly has a pathological dislike of anything that detracts from his own playing. He's been known to dismiss players from recordings if he thinks that their musical line might be intrusive. I experienced this at first-hand when I turned up for a concert at the Barbican to find the harpsichord had been removed following the rehearsal – I gather that my continuo part was distracting. I always found it fascinating that two of the most courteous conductors working in my earlier days, Sir John Pritchard and Sir Charles Groves, both spoke to me before rehearsing *Dance of the Sugar Plum Fairy* to ask how I liked to take it – hardly necessary, but a nice consideration.

To digress, and whilst talking about *Harry Potter,* which I was a while back – the first time I heard that magical 'celestial' opening to the first film was in a big music store in Manchester in 2001, where I was staying for some performances with the Hallé and my friend Stephen Bell. I had only recently given the first performance of my own Celeste Concertino with the BBCCO in a special broadcast of *Friday Night is Music Night* from the BBC's Maida Vale Studios and was unaware that there was any serious competition on the concerto front! That *Friday Night* (as it is known) was particularly poignant as my very dear friend, and longtime principal keyboard player of the Royal Philharmonic Orchestra (RPO) Vivian Troon, who at the time was very seriously ill, managed to get to the studio for the performance, together with his wife, Angela Fussell – the concertino is dedicated to them. Viv was appointed to the RPO many years earlier, having been engaged by a horn player as his accompanying pianist for an audition, in the presence of the orchestra's then music director, Rudolph Kempe. The horn player didn't find success, but Kempe asked Viv to stay behind, and he offered him the position of principal keyboard player – that's the way to do it! Viv passed away early in 2002, and I was honoured to be asked to deliver the eulogy at his funeral. He was a dear friend, and nearly twenty years on I still miss his company, good humour and sage advice.

From the mid-eighties, I had spent much time making sometimes daily visits to the BBC Concert Orchestra in Golders Green. The Hippodrome was the orchestra's base for many years, where it gave concerts and recorded programmes such as *Melodies for You*, *Matinée Musicales* and, of course, *Friday Night is Music Night*, in which I've worked with a range of amazing artists – I'm told I have appeared in a few hundred episodes.

A *Friday Night* would start with a piano rehearsal with the 'star singers' and the conductor. I should make a special mention of the great Robin Stapleton (an imposing figure and one-time chorus master at the Royal Opera House) who to my mind was the 'master' in that situation when it came to singers and operatic repertoire. These rehearsals could be great fun, especially when the wit and good humour of producers such as Alan Boyd and Bridget Apps were brought into the mix. For many years, the programme would also involve a small chorus, frequently the Nigel Brooks Singers but later there were groups such as Serenata Voices directed by David Bevan, the Stephen Hill Singers and the BBC Singers. The chorus would invariably sing in the finale of the show which, more often than not, would be a medley of show tunes arranged by one of the masters of that genre, such as Robert Docker or Gordon Langford.

For the first few years that I worked with the BBCCO, Ashley Lawrence was their much-loved principal conductor. A shy and somewhat retiring man, he would frequently sit quietly at the front of the studio during breaks, looking through the scores. He was quite philosophical by nature and if something wasn't quite perfect for a recording that would likely only ever be heard once on the radio, his reply to a request to rerecord a passage would often be, "Next time ..."

Ashley passed away unexpectedly whilst on tour in Japan and, in accordance with his wishes, he was buried in dress tails, together with a full score of Mahler's *Song of the Earth* and a bottle of Scotch. Barry Wordsworth followed Ashley as principal conductor and remains conductor laureate. A lovely man with great musical integrity, and also a fine keyboard player, Barry brings his own special musicianship to everything he performs. He and I have worked together countless times over the years, recording and performing many of the 'Denham' concertos such as *The Dream of Olwen*, *Cornish Rhapsody* and *Warsaw Concerto* with both the BBCCO and the RPO. The nickname for these pieces stems from the fact that the piano-featured scores for many of these films were recorded in the old Denham Studios.

The programming for *Friday Nights* was intriguingly varied – you could easily slide from a show tune to a piece of Messiaen via Bach. Most shows had a brace of vocal soloists and usually a solo instrumentalist. Frequently that soloist came from within the orchestra, but sometimes a 'superstar' would be brought in. On one occasion, the eminent American organist Carlo Curley, by then resident in the UK, was engaged, together with his concert organ. A larger-than-life character, Carlo was found by the main entrance five minutes before the start of the live Radio 2 broadcast, shaking hands with each audience member as they arrived and introducing himself, saying, "Hello, I'm Carlo Curley, your organist tonight." Meanwhile, the management was apoplectic with panic!

It would be invidious to list all the celebrated musicians who have come to join the programme over the years, spanning the gamut of styles from classical to pop, via jazz and musical theatre. Just occasionally an artiste would leave us scratching our heads. One such star was the pianist Einaudi, who joined the orchestra for a *Friday Night* from LSO St

Luke's – the LSO's fabulous rehearsal/performance venue just north of the Barbican and housing one of the loveliest pianos I know.

Maybe he didn't bring his best repertoire with him, but it seemed as though he sat at the piano playing a succession of very basic chords, repeating for some five minutes, and leaving most of my colleagues very puzzled. We were clearly missing something, as he sells out concert halls, receives rave reviews and is worth a fortune. What I found unacceptable was that, when taking over from me at the piano, he roughly shoved me off the piano-stool before I'd even finished my final chord!

I would frequently be asked to contribute a piano solo to these broadcasts, and sometimes, if a live programme was running a little late, the producer would appear behind a window or at a side door, mid-solo, gesturing frantically to make a cut. I remember on one occasion managing to get Chopin's *Minute Waltz* down to around forty seconds … almost not worth starting! Occasionally a personal friend would turn up for a performance, which was always a special pleasure, and I remember the greatly loved Lindsay Benson making many appearances as baritone soloist, Bramwell Tovey (now principal conductor) would conduct, and Julia Wilson-James would frequently appear with the BBC Singers. Presenters for the show, in my time, have included Robin Boyle, Richard Baker, Brian Kay, Aled Jones, Ken Bruce and Paul Gambaccini.

My wife Jo once mentioned to a friend that I was featuring on a *Friday Night*. He had a great deal of experience in the performing arts and responded by saying, "I'm guessing he'll be getting at least a thousand pounds for that." This highlights one of the great misconceptions of working in classical music. Possibly the case for some of those working on the 'glamorous' pop side of our business, but the reality in situations such as mine is that the fees are a fraction of this. There simply isn't the money in the classical arena; at least, not for those of us essentially on the shop floor!

Back in the eighties and nineties, there were frequent weekend trips to various parts of the country. These would usually involve a *Friday Night* followed by a Saturday-night gala concert. In fact, we did quite a bit of travelling at that time, and we would happily drive to somewhere like Llandudno or Newcastle for a rehearsal and broadcast and then home

Sir Roger Norrington, Elgar *Cockaigne* • LPO • Prom (August 1996)

afterwards. I remember on one occasion, the orchestra was in Falmouth and we had broken the journey the day before, stopping in Exeter overnight. However, the day after the concert many of us were due to be at Marble Hill House, Richmond for an outdoor concert with that master conductor, Sir Edward Heath, battling, as always, through Elgar's *Cockaigne* overture. Several of us drove back through the night – I shared a car with Alistair Young, and we drove an hour on and an hour off, eventually finding sleep at around 4:00am I think. I really wouldn't want to do that now! Talking of *Cockaigne,* there's an interesting quirk at the cut-off near the end of the piece – the organ is given longer note lengths than the rest of the orchestra, and it's somewhat ambiguous as to whether the organ holds through the orchestra's silence. To my way of thinking, this is very effective, and when I queried it with Sir Roger Norrington ahead of a Prom with the LPO, he agreed that we do it that way, and to great dramatic effect in the RAH. Perhaps Elgar intended an organ feature – maybe it's simply an error in the score ...

It's interesting to think back to the days of out-of-town concerts and the little traditions for stopping on the way home for a nightcap – the whole drink-driving culture has changed considerably. I've never been a big drinker, but I would stop, to be sociable, maybe near junction eighteen of the M4 on the way back from Cardiff or, quite frequently, junction twelve of the M1 at the Sow and Pigs in Toddington. In those days the timpanist was Bernard Davis – a clever chap although somewhat prone to taking unscheduled personal breaks in rehearsal. I got on very well with him and would sometimes share a car with him and Jan Parr, the fixer. Bernard came loaded with many lives when it came to drinking and driving, and there are several stories of him running off the road after a post-concert drink and on at least one occasion being helped back to safety by passing emergency services without any questions. I remember being with him and a few others in the Sow and Pigs one evening, late to the point that we were 'locked in'. We were standing in a group; Bernard with his back to the open fire. I imagine that he had been drinking for much of the day because at one point, he slid slowly, and without apparent concern, down into the blazing fire (and was pulled out pretty quickly!)

There were also a good many foreign trips with the BBCCO to some quite exotic locations. The first for me was the amazing 1987 trip to Hong Kong. We literally dropped into the old Kai Tak airport, having flown down the High Street, past the washing hanging from the balconies of the high-rise accommodation blocks on each side, skirted the flyover at the end of the runway and then bumped onto the tarmac! I had been hoping that we would make this legendary approach to Kai Tak and I wasn't disappointed. We stayed in Sha Tin in the New Territories but spent any free time commuting to Kowloon and also crossing to Hong Kong Island to visit as much as possible.

One evening, Stephen Bell and I had planned to meet up with some of the orchestra in one of Hong Kong's oldest and best-loved bars, Ned Kelly's Last Stand. However, before that we were curious to take a look at the legendary Bottoms Up club, famously featured in the Bond movie *The Man with the Golden Gun*. Standing at the hotel reception waiting for the shuttle bus, we were joined by Jan Parr, longtime orchestra fixer and a good friend. Also Georgina Rice-Oxley (PA to David Rayvern Allen, the Radio 2 producer when not writing books on cricket). They asked where we were going – we told them we were heading into town and they asked if they could join us. It would have been churlish to refuse, but we were not about to be deterred from pursuing our inquisitive natures. We duly arrived at the club, went downstairs to the bar and ordered drinks. Full marks to the girls – they joined in the 'spirit' of the occasion and not a word was mentioned about our choice of watering hole!

This was a short, exhausting, but fabulous trip. Back at the airport for the return flight, some of the double-bass section had, naturally, acquired an inflatable gorilla, which aroused quite a bit of interest from the security staff when let loose close to the gate. I gather there was even more excitement at Heathrow when security staff spotted the gorilla's feet sticking out of the luggage belonging to the then principal bass, Roderick Dunk!

Roderick Dunk and friend • Kai Tak airport, HK (1987)

There was a memorable occasion in the late eighties when I joined Rod and some members of the BBCSO for a lunchtime foyer concert in the RFH. We were playing Schubert's piano quintet *The Trout* and, quite unusually, the publicity indicated two Rodericks – Roderick Dunk, double bass, closely followed by myself. What made that performance particularly demanding was the presence of friends and colleagues from the London Philharmonic Orchestra (LPO) who had wandered down to the foyer in their lunch break to see what was going on! You don't often find a Rash of Rodericks, but there was a funny occasion some years earlier when there had actually been four of us on stage at the Barbican for an LSO concert, resulting in a fair degree of confusion during rehearsal. Rod left the orchestra in 1990 to pursue a very successful career as a conductor.

A few years after the Hong Kong trip, I was in the USA in the middle of an RPO tour but had decided to fly back, when not needed mid-tour, in order to undertake a BBCCO concert in Istanbul, which I'd not visited. We stayed in the Hilton, at that time one of the top listed hotels in the world and located high up overlooking the Bosporus. I remember waking early on the first morning to see the sun shimmering on this magical and evocative strip of water marking the boundary between Europe and Asia. Time was limited, and I joined the horns for a whistle-stop taxi tour of the city, taking in the Blue Mosque, the famous covered market and copious amounts of Turkish coffee – sleep had been at a premium, as so frequently on tour; in this case because of a very late departure due to problems with Turkish Airlines.

As always, there was great company with this lovely group. The rehearsal was a curiosity – it contained a violin concerto, which was being ferociously attacked by a local player whom, I think, the BBCCO members thought to be in danger of causing grave damage to his violin. In fact, the inevitable did happen, and with some drama, the poor chap's tail-gut broke. This is the piece of (usually) thick nylon that takes the full tension of the string assembly. It was quite an explosion! After this excitement, I flew back to join the RPO tour, now in Miami and ready for a little more two-keyboard action with Vivian Troon.

A trip to Stockholm arose in 2001 – this was something of 'Coals to Newcastle' as one of our outdoor concerts was completely devoted to the music of ABBA. I particularly enjoyed this, as I have always been a fan! With me was Andy Vinter, a lovely pianist with a specialism for lighter music and who can seemingly turn his hands to any style. I also had a great deal of fun discovering many interesting and hitherto undiscovered sounds on a synthesizer! It appears that the audience was similarly delighted and we could clearly do no wrong. There was a degree of embarrassment in the hotel however – being summer, and the sun never really setting, a large percentage of the orchestra remained on the terrace doing their best to assuage their seemingly endless thirst. On this occasion, it took a particularly long time, lasting well into the early hours and totally draining the resources of the hotel bar. We suspected that this hotel had not previously entertained a British orchestra.

There was also a trip to Spain for Mendelssohn's *Elijah* – notable for the soloist being taken ill and the piece becoming Elijah minus one (also memorable for all the orchestral return flight tickets being packed in the manager's luggage). There were wonderful tours with Barry Wordsworth to the USA as well as two fantastic tours to Japan, all under the supportive and guiding influence of the orchestra's esteemed manager, Adrian Evett. One particularly anxious moment occurred on the second tour (2002) when a patch of crimson started to spread across the front of Barry's white dress shirt, causing at least one member of the orchestra to faint! I think that with our collective and creative imaginations, we had all been having flashbacks to a scene from one of the James Bond films

'Musical highlight of the day' with horn section, Stockholm (2001)

where someone is shot from a blowpipe – of course, the reality was far less fanciful. That tour programme featured the new orchestral suite from *Harry Potter* with its famous celeste solo, and from early on in the trip, the Japanese road crew would greet me with, "Ah, Meester Potter!"

It was for such 'out-of-town' adventures that I appreciated the support and friendship of the orchestra's 'crew'; not just for keeping my music in order and helping to transport my keyboard equipment when needed, but also for keeping me greatly entertained after hours. The photo below was taken during a rather fun expedition for a televised concert from Cardiff Arms Park, for which the orchestra was joined by Sir Willard White, Leslie Garrett, Russell Watson and Robin Stapleton. They are (left to right) Eunice Brushfield-Hodges (librarian) and her husband Terry, Michael Cousins (transport), Brian Grogan (stage manager) and Scott Jones (transport, and later stage manager).

Since its inception in 1991, I was the official pianist for the BBC Radio 2 Young Musician competition, which was responsible for the launching of many careers. Applicants recorded a piece in the Maida Vale Studios and also a short interview with presenter Leonard Pearcey. These recordings were then auditioned by a panel of judges, and a shortlist was drawn up for inclusion in a series of eight programmes, with two performers in each. These broadcasts were auditioned, and from the sixteen competitors, a final was drawn up, which took place in London's Queen Elizabeth Hall. The finalists were partnered by the BBCCO and conductor Andrew Greenwood. Sadly this competition ended in 2001, following which, Radio 2 diversified into other, more specific types of young musician awards.

The stars of the BBC support team at Cardiff Arms Park – Eunice, Terry, Mike, Brian and Scott (2002)

For many years Radio 2 ran a fifteen-minute programme called *At the Piano,* for which I was invited to contribute several recitals – the first such invitation coming from Radio 2 producer Tim McDonald, who had previously worked as a producer for Decca. Tim was blessed with a terrific sense of humour, and he and I had some great times together over the years, not least when a bass drum caught fire during a rehearsal in the Royal College of Music!

Tim McDonald, Radio 2, windy Weymouth (1994)

Given the relatively short length of *At the Piano,* two episodes would be recorded during a standard three-hour recording slot (most engagements in the music profession are based on three-hour blocks). I remember on one occasion turning up for the second half of a session in Maida Vale Studio 6 and finding myself following the great Rick Wakeman.

When I first started recording these programmes, we were usually in Studio 3 at Maida Vale. This studio had been designed for the BBC Radio Orchestra and Big Band and, to my mind, was not ideal for classical piano recording due to its very dry acoustic. I asked whether we could investigate using the more classically-orientated Studio 2 next door (also the home of the BBC Singers) and this we did regularly, the studio giving a lovely bloom to the piano. We had a great deal of fun with those recordings, and once, I asked to bring my colleague John Alley to play a second piano. It was for this Christmas episode that I wrote my *Christmas Mudley* for two pianos, each player also playing a celeste. Well, it looked impressive …

I was told by a producer that on one occasion, he broke his own rule of never booking anyone for *At the Piano* on the basis of an audition tape having been sent in. Apparently, a particular recording had sounded so impressive that he engaged the gentleman without further consideration. As my father regularly used to say, there's no such thing as a free lunch – pretty much the first thing this pianist said when he arrived in the studio was, "Which stave do you want me to record first?" – clearly intent on using both hands to record each of the right- and left-hand parts and laying one recording on top of the other!

One of the last *At the Piano*s I recorded was a whim of the producer, who wanted me to play Beethoven's *Moonlight* Sonata. Due to timing constraints, and the musical demands of the last movement, I recorded that movement first, followed by the middle movement. We then worked out how much time we had left and divided it by the number of bars and beats required for the first movement in order to calculate a suitable metronome mark. We set a silent 'click' going on a metronome and off we went, ending up just under fifteen minutes. Incidentally, that recording was made in the old Concert Hall of Broadcasting House which, at the time, was one of the finest chamber-music venues the BBC had. Unfortunately, it was decided to convert the hall into a Radio Theatre, which pretty much destroyed the acoustic as it was.

Occasionally one project leads to another when you least expect it ... when I was fifty seconds short for an *At the Piano* recital, I wrote a very short piece reminiscent of cascading water and, in haste, called it *Aquarius*. As I left the studio (Maida Vale Studio 4), the producer Maura Clarke called after me, "Just eleven to go!" That was the beginning of *Twelve Astrological Preludes*. Another occasion comes to mind when I had just broadcast a new piano solo from Golders Green called *A Little Fall-ish!* – one of the few pieces that have just come without thought. I wrote it shortly after watching the funeral of Diana, Princess of Wales on television – without a doubt, this short piece reflects the mood of the occasion. This was dedicated to an American friend, and the title is a nod to the fact that autumn leaves were falling and the American for autumnal might be fall-ish. Following the broadcast, my friend Stephen Bell, then principal horn of the BBCCO, came into the dressing room playing the opening phrase of my new piece, clearly showing that I had written it for the wrong instrument! In many ways he was right, and I immediately set about orchestrating this piece for solo horn and chamber orchestra, which we then broadcast on a *Friday Night*. This movement was followed each 'term' by another until I had a complete set of four 'seasons', which were subsequently published under the title *Four Seasonal Nocturnes*. I had always wanted to write a fifth movement called *Silly Season,* but that's not yet arrived!

I first met Steve in 1984 when he came to audition for the orchestra as fourth horn, and while he was still on the postgraduate conducting course at the RCM. We hit it off straightaway, and he played a sensational audition – one of the most sensitive and intuitive horn players I've ever known. He later moved up the section to become principal horn, where he remained for many years. We were to share countless meals together – meals that we affectionately nicknamed the 'musical highlight of the day'! However, Steve was always destined to conduct, ultimately relinquishing his position with the BBC in 2015 and hanging up his horn for good following a performance of Elgar's *Enigma Variations* with Barry Wordsworth in The Maltings, Snape.

I've probably always had a latent love affair with the cor anglais, but I don't think this showed itself until back in 2000, when I made an arrangement of the Sinfonia from J.S. Bach's Cantata 29. I found myself making quite a feature of this instrument, which was played by my dear friend Victoria Walpole, the cor anglais player for the BBCCO and next to whom the piano was generally situated in the final years that the orchestra was based in Golders Green. The broadcast of this was to be the last occasion that my parents could get to the studio. They were very supportive of all that I did, and I used to value looking up to the balcony during a concert to see their smiling faces. This interest in the cor anglais led me to write a complete piece for Vicky called *Cygncopations*. This new piece, with chamber orchestra, was premiered by her as part of a cor anglais-featured *Friday Night* from London's Mermaid Theatre in July 2003, conducted by Robin Stapleton. Incidentally, Robin's name has the distinction of a splendid anagram, *Boris P. Notalent,* which couldn't be less appropriate – a legacy from master anagramist, the ex-timpanist Bernard Davis.

The rehearsal for this occasion was especially memorable … I had given Robin a copy of the score several weeks earlier to take with him to Italy. He was always particular about knowing his scores properly. Similarly, I can be particular about the markings in my scores, especially if I feel they are not being adhered to! It was therefore somewhat challenging when I heard Robin start to rehearse *Cygncopations* radically slower than indicated in the score. With the respect I have for Robin's musicianship I bit my tongue and remained calm. As the movement progressed, I actually saw what Robin had found – a gradual increase of pace on each repetition of the main theme. Whilst this was not how I had conceived it, I actually liked this fresh idea to the point that I said nothing to Robin and subsequently revised the score accordingly. That is the version that was published and recorded. The work has been played several times since by the BBCCO and also recorded by Vicky with the RPO on my album *A Little Fall-ish!* Incidentally, the swan (*cygne*) reference is due to there being a famous piece by Sibelius called *The Swan of Tuonela* that features the cor anglais as a swan. Also, my piece is hugely influenced by the musical device of syncopation. I subsequently arranged both *Cygncopations* and its companion piece, *Il Cygnet*, for saxophone with either piano or chamber orchestra, and I'm delighted that *Cygncopations* has been included in the ABRSM Grade 8 saxophone syllabus for some years.

The BBCCO formally left the Hippodrome in 2003 and, for the most part, was presenting concerts from the Mermaid Theatre in Blackfriars, a stone's throw from my old school and even closer to the new CLS building. There had been several issues during the final years at Golders Green, not least two serious ceiling collapses – luckily both at night-time, when the building was closed, otherwise the implications for the horn section and principal cellist, Nigel Blomiley, would have been grave. We missed our two favourite restaurants – the Local Friends Chinese immediately opposite the theatre and L'Artista, the famous Italian restaurant just under the railway bridge. However, as is the way of these things, we grew to enjoy the abundance of new eating establishments discovered in the City of London, not least Harry's Bar and its pizzas.

In 2006, Sir Richard Rodney Bennett celebrated his seventieth birthday with the orchestra with a concert for Radio 3 from London's Queen Elizabeth Hall. This was a special occasion that included his Concerto

Robin Stapleton, Alan Boyd and Victoria Walpole after *Cygncopations* (July 2003)

for Stan Getz (which the orchestra had previously played at a Prom with Barry Wordsworth and saxophonist John Harle). On this occasion, it was played by the saxophonist Andy Scott. The evening ended with Richard playing the concertante piano solo from his score for *Murder on the Orient Express*. Earlier, Richard had joined me at the piano for the orchestral piano-duet part in his magical suite from the film *Far from the Madding Crowd*. He was quite insistent that as he didn't play the piano so much, I should play the top part. I'm not sure I agreed with this statement, but it was a gracious gesture. At the break, we had a fascinating conversation about approaches to composition, especially regarding working at the piano. I've long felt that writing at the keyboard can be inhibiting, at least for me, and it was interesting to hear Richard's thoughts. We both felt that when working on something at the keyboard, it's all too easy for the hands to move in set patterns from familiar muscular memory – not allowing free rein to the imagination. I just wish that my own moments of inspiration didn't frequently seem to come in the middle the night!

In more recent years, the orchestra and Radio 3 developed a close relationship with the late Sir Stephen Cleobury and King's College, Cambridge, where they have undertaken a number of concerts and broadcasts, frequently at Easter. My last visit there was for a special performance given prior to the removal and refurbishment of the famous organ. The concert included a performance of Saint-Saëns' *Organ Symphony*, for which I was joined by my wife Jo for the delightful piano-duet section. The legendary Thomas Trotter, an ex-King's organ scholar, was making all the noise on that occasion. Some years earlier there had been a plan afoot for me and Thomas to make a recording of French repertoire for piano and organ, but sadly, due to changes in management and personnel, the plan didn't come to fruition. The Harrison & Harrison organ in King's was removed immediately after the 2015 Christmas services, with the tight time-constraint of needing to be back in place, fully voiced and working reliably, in good time for the annual Service of Nine Lessons and Carols on Christmas Eve 2016. It would have been unthinkable for the instrument not to be available for that famous occasion.

I have made several references in this book to Saint-Saëns' *Organ Symphony*, actually his Symphony No. 3 in C minor. This is extremely popular, and rightly so. It is beautifully crafted by Saint-Saëns at what was probably the peak of his career. The work is not, as sometimes presented, an organ concerto, but a symphony in four sections (within two movements) with an organ appearing in two of them – in effect, an orchestral organ part. The first of the organ sections (the slow movement) is an absolute gem, written to embrace some of the gentler sounds of the instrument, which merge so beautifully with the orchestral textures.

Of course, the famous moment is the appearance of the organ at the start of the final section, where temptation is to utilise the whole battery of power available to the organist, rather than the more modest *forte*, indicated by Saint-Saëns. Quite frequently, this request comes from the promoter or conductor, who feel they want to satisfy the expectations of the audience, rather than the composer! My organist colleague Stephen Farr has the perfect answer to this, "Well, you conduct *fortissimo* and I'll play what Saint-Saëns wrote." When played as such, the organist does not show his full hand until the apocalyptic ending, where he goes into battle with the full orchestral forces and solo timpanist.

Mention should be made of Saint-Saëns' idiomatic piano writing. The third section (the scherzo) employs something of a concertante style of writing, with rapid scales and arpeggios. This section can, on occasion, be challenging when a conductor does not maintain a stable tempo or, indeed, sets off at a speed that is totally inappropriate. In the final section, following the loud organ chords, there is an exquisitely gentle section for strings and piano-duet, where two pianists play rippling arpeggios using all four hands across the entire length of the piano keyboard, providing a unique and captivating texture.

It's always uplifting to make music in inspiring settings such as King's College, and another favourite building which the BBCCO has visited frequently in recent years is Dorchester Abbey. This is the home of the English Music Festival where the BBCCO has presented some interestingly diverse and previously unperformed repertoire, under the perceptive direction of Martin Yates with whom I've also had the pleasure of making a number of recordings over the years. The abbey is host to a very fine organ, most recently overhauled by the firm of Peter Collins, and on my last visit I used it to add substantial weight to Martin's reconstruction of Montague Phillips' Symphony in C minor. The first time I walked into the abbey (2015) was something of a shock, as there in front of me was a billboard with a life-size photo of my old friend Brian Kay. The bass in the original King's Singers, Brian had a close relationship with the BBC, for many years presenting *Friday Night is Music Night* for Radio 2 as well as *Brian Kay's Light Programme* and *3 for All* for Radio 3. I first met Brian in 1988 when playing the famous organ in Huddersfield Town Hall for a BBC broadcast with the Huddersfield Choral Society. What a chorus and what an organ! I got to know quite a few of the choir and my piano intermezzo *Gazelle* is dedicated to one of them, Dorcas Owen. This is from a set of three intermezzi – the second being *A little Fall-ish!* and the final one *Elegie*, based on the Irish folk song 'She moved through the fair'. I started this shortly after my father was admitted to hospital in 2001, finishing it a few days after he passed away. It's dedicated to his memory.

My long and close relationship with the BBC has embraced many special opportunities and experiences, and the adventures have been amazing. I have learned a huge amount about a diversity of repertoire, visited some wonderful places, made many recordings and countless good friends – these I will always treasure. However, I can't leave discussion of performances for the BBC without making mention of 'that' Prom in August 2003, for which my co-pianist and good friend Alistair

Brian Kay welcoming us to Dorchester Abbey (May 2015)

Martin Yates & the BBCCO in Dorchester Abbey (May 2015)

Young and I dressed up as schoolboys for the solo piano-duet feature in Malcolm Arnold's suite from *The Belles of St Trinian's*. There was some discussion that we would dress up as schoolgirls, in deference to the film. However, I think that the then director of the Proms, Nicholas Kenyon, had issues with such prominent cross-dressing, so the wearing of boaters with attached pigtails was left to the irrepressible Alasdair Malloy and his band of percussionists. We devised a little pantomime to get ourselves onstage, along with 'headmaster' Rumon Gamba, following our introduction from Timothy West. This included the music being delivered upside down and my firing a catapult at the conductor – probably the only time that I will legally be allowed to do so! Before Alistair and I went on, I said that the last thing I must do is to forget my glasses and as you can see from the video in the moment before we play, that's precisely what I did!

With 'headmaster' Rumon Gamba and Alistair Young, *The Belles of St Trinian's* (August 2013)

8 – Orchestral Auditions

Soon after starting to work with the BBCCO I began to get requests to act as an audition pianist when such situations arose with both the BBCCO, the BBCSO and, in the early days until its disbandment, the BBC Radio Orchestra. Like the BBCSO, the Radio Orchestra was based at the BBC's Maida Vale Studios in west London – mostly working in Studio 3. The BBC has an enlightened approach to orchestral auditions and invariably engages two accompanying pianists. Apart from being good socially, this also allows the maximum amount of rehearsal time which is better for both the candidate and the pianist. Auditions usually vary in length from ten to twenty minutes, and when there's just one pianist and any distance to walk from rehearsal room to the audition, there's not much time to rehearse, if any. Sometimes it's just a hasty word at the door about the speed of the pieces.

My first day of auditions was for the BBCCO at the Hippodrome, and I felt honoured to find myself joined by that doyenne of accompanying pianists, Daphne Ibbott. Daphne was an absolute darling from whom I learned a great deal about the nature and psychology of audition accompaniment. One of the finest pianists of her generation, she was in considerable demand by many of the great artists of the day, such as the violinists Alfredo Campoli, Nona Liddell and Felix Kok, as well as the singers John Carol Case and David Johnston. I remember going to the RAM to hear her in recital, I believe with Derek Collier. Their recital concluded with an exhilarating performance of Ravel's notoriously challenging *Tzigane*, which was dashed off with huge aplomb.

The other reason for my great excitement at meeting Daphne was historic – for years as a young boy I would sit with Mum and listen to the daily Radio 4 broadcast *Listen With Mother*. I was always delighted to hear a name-check for the pianist Daphne Ibbott, although her name was not significant to me at the time. This programme also introduced me, subconsciously, to the uniquely unsettling sound of the augmented triad – something you'll understand if you've ever heard the signature tune! Daphne was married to the flautist and harp-maker Wilfred Smith, whom she frequently joined for flute and piano recitals.

Daphne had not been able to join us for quite a few years before she passed away in 2002. Most usually for BBC audition days, I would then be paired with John Alley, Alistair Young, Marion Lee, Winnie Wu or Michael Round. Most other

Alfredo Campoli in recital with Daphne Ibbott, United Church of Egham (May 1972)

orchestras have a rather different approach to auditions, with only one accompanying pianist being engaged.

Audition days can be challenging, as well as very rewarding. They frequently run later than scheduled, and stipulated breaks can magically disappear. Audition panels vary drastically in their approach to time-keeping. No one likes to stop a candidate mid-performance, but in reality, that's how it has to be. There are formal agreements as to how pianists should be engaged for audition accompanying, and this is to safeguard standards as well as to keep pianists sane and protect their fees. So often now these details are simply ignored or possibly adjusted creatively to suit the finances of the organisation concerned – frequently without consultation of the poor pianist. The pianist is then put in the position of having to decide whether to ignore the situation, to their own disadvantage, or to point out the issue of overtime or lack of a break, with the adherent fear of being branded a troublemaker and not being asked back. I have to say that I don't remember this approach back in the eighties, when the organisation of time and payment always seemed to be processed correctly and fairly. I'm not sure whether this is a by-product of our computer era, organisations not properly instructing junior staff, or the hope of saving money (I know, I'm an old cynic!).

No one is at their best if they unexpectedly find themselves forced to sit at a piano for several hours without a break and maintain a fully professional level of performance and accompanimental support. Unfortunately, it does happen, and on rare occasions you will even find timetables that have been produced indicating no breaks at all.

One symphony orchestra in London had a bad reputation for engaging audition pianists for a whole day of auditions, then telling them at the last minute that they were now only occupying, and paying for, a couple of hours – sometimes across the middle of the day. This situation is unacceptable on three counts, of course – firstly this takes out the whole of the day, as you cannot now work elsewhere in either the morning or the afternoon, and other work may well have been turned down. Secondly, you cannot, strictly, cancel or change a booking at such short notice and thirdly, there is a three-hour minimum call, which some people seem reluctant to understand. The principle of this is quite simple and is an attempt to give some acknowledgement to the fact that there is essential travelling time and expense involved in every engagement. As this is not usually reimbursed when working within the M25, travel costs can seriously impact on a fee – all the more so if someone is expecting to pay you for just one or two hours. This probably sounds as though I'm very money-centric, which I really don't think I am. Making music is not a conventional job – it's broadly a passion that delivers great rewards, not all financial. However, part of that reward needs to be the wherewithal to pay for a roof over your head and food to eat!

I always felt that you need to quickly assess the 'mental state' of the applicant with whom you are about to rehearse. People can be exceedingly anxious in this situation and sometimes quite aggressive. I think it's easy for us to not fully understand the considerable stress of going into a solo performance situation in front of colleagues, many of whom will be far more experienced than yourself, as well as holding a position of power over you in terms of whether they progress you through the application process. The format for most instrumental auditions is to play the first movement of a Mozart concerto (assuming he wrote one for the relevant instrument; another standard if he didn't) and the first movement of any concerto from the romantic repertoire. I have encountered a few puzzling situations over the years whilst playing for orchestral auditions. These have highlighted the degree of commitment, time-keeping and integrity that need to be brought into preparing for such an occasion. I'm repeating four of them as cautionary tales, and they are not intended in any way to be disrespectful.

The first concerned a viola player who turned up late for her audition. She was flustered, refused to rehearse and quickly disappeared to the loo – when she returned, we went straight into the audition. En route, I asked what her free choice was. "The Walton," she said, which she wanted to play first. This is pretty standard repertoire that had come up several times earlier that day. She refused further conversation. We went in, she tuned, and I started at the beginning, as is invariable with this work. Big mistake ... she stopped me, barking, "No, the second movement." If you know the work, you will appreciate the implications for sight-reading this piece with absolutely no preparation. The poor girl was then in more of a state through a simple lack of communication.

This was closely followed by the chap who turned up to play Wieniawski's Polonaise in D major for Violin. From my perhaps limited experience of a polonaise, I had anticipated this to be performed with the usual three beats in a bar. Unfortunately, he had a unique approach to the work and proceeded to play it with *four* beats in a bar. There was no shaking him, so I conceded defeat and we headed down to the audition to perform it with an extra beat in each bar. I rather feared what lay ahead, especially knowing the make-up of the audition panel awaiting us. We made a start, but it wasn't long before the panel was, inevitably, struggling – a difficult situation for my colleagues, whose handkerchieves had come out to cover the awkwardness. I have no idea whether the auditionee was aware, but he struggled on valiantly until the panel's chairman, also the leader of the orchestra, interrupted to ask the auditionee, in his broad Welsh accent, whether he had brought anything else.

"The Mozart D major Concerto," he said with some confidence, "but could I play it without the piano as it puts me off?"

Fair comment I thought and got up to leave. The chairman's retort to me "Rod, let that be a lesson to you!"

Then there was the extremely rude young lady who came to audition for a first violin position. We started to rehearse the free choice, the Brahms' Concerto. Now, in my experience, the general principle of concerto accompaniment is that, where practical, the pianist follows what the soloist is doing in respect of movement and dynamics. However, I clearly had something to learn – her performance became more and more erratic until eventually, she stopped and said, "Why are you f***ing about?"

"Excuse me?" I said. "I can't follow you," was her reply. I tried to point out to her that maybe she had the wrong concept of what should be happening here and that I didn't appreciate her language. She huffed, and we carried on without further comment – quite extraordinary! I'm sure she was nervous and maybe somewhat out of her depth, but even so ...

Possibly the most curious anecdote of all is the young man who attended a first violin audition with an arguably lightweight programme of Mozart's G major Concerto and Kreisler's Praeludium and Allegro. For the most part, the audition was highly undistinguished. What made this situation particularly puzzling was that the chap's CV said that he had worked for one of our leading symphony orchestras, a detail which, after a few moments of performance, was being noted between the panel members with some disbelief. At the break, I made enquiries of a friend working in the office of the orchestra in question, and it turned out that this chap had once driven the orchestra's lorry on tour. So, although he had not strictly fibbed, he'd clearly not thought through his unusual strategy for achieving success!

Candidates will occasionally turn up without any piano parts, perhaps assuming that you have copies of every possible concerto in your bag. Others bring loose sheets of photocopies – illegal to play from, of course, and creating havoc on the music desk for page-turning, sometimes ending up on the floor.

I've used the phrase 'accompanying pianist'. I know that I'm not alone in feeling that the term accompanist is something of a malapropism in the context of much of the instrumental music we get asked to play. So often a piece will be billed as say, Brahms' Sonata in A for Violin, when the title is actually Sonata in A for Violin *and Piano* – the violin and piano parts being equal, both musically and technically. To describe the pianist's role in this situation as an accompanist seems somewhat demeaning.

9 – Gnaff Days

Towards the end of the seventies, a group of us with a similarly misguided sense of humour formed ourselves into the internationally unknown Gnaff Ensemble, giving many performances to packed-out concert halls all over ~~the world~~ Essex. The members were:

Bramwell Tovey (composer/vocals/tuba/piano/saxophone)
Paul Hart (composer/jazz violin/jazz piano/synth/double bass)
Christopher Stearn (lyricist extraordinaire/bass trombone)
Russell Jordan (drums/tuned percussion/coiled spring)
Howard Sim (trumpet/programme/music copyist)
Roderick Elms (keyboards/double bass/composer/technician)

Some of the immortal titles we performed included *Eine Kleine Gnaffmusik, The Rewrite of Spring*, and *Concerto Gross*. Colleagues were 'queuing up' to join us when forces demanded, such as for orchestral based concerts and our legendary big-band shows, featuring leading London jazz players and Lindsay Benson on vocals. Not literally queuing up, of course, but musical friends travelled great distances to join in our madcap antics. It was also encouraging that our sell-out concerts received surprisingly good reviews. Our most popular shows were:

Less Brass, More Polish; Gnaff Flying High; The Gnaff Mystery Show; The Gnaff Ensemble Straightens Out; Gnaff Christmas Extravaganza; The Gnaff Ensemble Spring Clean; The Gnaff Ensemble Grand Outing; Quintessential Gnaff; Gnaff Ancient & Modern and *The Gnaff Package Tour.*

One Sunday afternoon, at the invitation of Geoffrey Timms of Ongar Music Club, the Gnaffs gave an afternoon performance to the unsuspecting children of Ongar, in Essex. We decided at an early stage of planning that we would present the world premiere of the hitherto unknown *Ongar Conga*. Traditionally, this involved a raucous procession out of the main doors, crossing Banson's Lane, right round the Sainsbury's car park and back in the rear doors of the hall – much to the delight of all concerned. This proved to be a highly popular item in the programme, although that may also have been its last performance.

In the summer of 1982, we recorded our first (and last) single at CBS Studios in London's Whitfield Street. We had great fun working on this, and the result was remarkable. Aficionados will know that for *Free Kings* we included the extended refrain, which is not always performed. This involved Paul and Bram, who pioneered a vocal technique known as *compressione nasale* for the words "and a queen".

This proved to be remarkably effective, and you can see it in action in the session photograph (page 72). This recording was released as our Christmas single on Ffang Records in 1982. It did get some airplay on Radio 1 and, we understand, many rave reviews, although we've never seen

Bram performing on the newfangled Electric Cor Anglais.

them. We also recorded *Free Kings* for ITV – broadcast on Boxing Day of that year and sharing the billing with The Krankies and Bananarama. Listening to this legendary track, you will appreciate the unbounded enthusiasm of the singers in reaching their home destination at Seven Kings. The 'B' side contained a spectacular arrangement of 'God Rest You Merry, Gentlemen' by Paul Hart, which is definitely worth a listen if you can get hold of a copy. At Easter 1982, the group went on a study weekend to Aldeburgh, staying on that occasion in the White Lion Hotel (inexplicably painted pink at the time – suitably gnaff, I suppose). One might say that the greeting from the manageress, Mrs Stitt, was a little on the cool side as the numbers arriving fell way short of the number of rooms booked. Somehow Bram managed to placate her, although he didn't himself arrive until the following morning. We booked a local hall in order to brainstorm ideas for our forthcoming world tour, but although

Gnaff training course with supporting friends • Cathy Giles, Russell Jordan, Clive Miller, Jane Miller, Bramwell Tovey, Paul Hart, Sue Eversden, Louise Stearn, Harold Sim, Christopher Stearn and Francesca Smith (c/w from bottom centre) • White Lion Hotel, Aldeburgh (April 1982)

Our first, and last, Christmas single (1982)

Paul Hart mixing *Free Kings* with Andy at CBS (1982)

we developed some new and what would undoubtedly be ground-breaking routines, we rather fell short of what we would need, so we had no choice but to downsize the tour considerably and drown our sorrows in the Cross Keys.

All the shows had quite diverse titles that broadly reflected some aspect of the content, such as *Gnaff Ancient and Modern* and *The Gnaff Package Tour,* for which the members stripped down to beachwear for a unique rendition of *The Carnival of the Animals* – this had to be heard (and seen) to be believed. We also recruited a number of local singers to form the *Gnaffharmonic Festival Chorus,* and they joined us on several occasions to perform some of our immortal charts which, of course, included *Carmina Biriani.*

Paul and Bram demonstrating *compressione nasale* (August 1982)

The secret Gnaff bar in Hainault Road. Chris, Howard, Bram, Paul and Rod (early '80s)

We did, in fact, rehearse, but before rehearsals could start there would always be a fairly strict period of research and adjustment. This, for the most part, was something of a *rituelle-gnaffe* that began in the Nightingale in Wanstead. When we left, somewhat after closing time (and frequently leaving behind pints of beer that had been bought for Russell, who had not turned up), we would head to the local Indian restaurant, the Rajdoot Tandoori, where plans would continue to evolve. These would ultimately be formalised in the cellar of Paul's home in Hainault Road, Leytonstone – a peaceful haven where we felt comfortable and safe to work, and where we could give free rein to our fermenting ideas. Late-night refreshments would frequently be accompanied by a little solid sustenance, provided by Paul's wife, Cathy.

The Gnaff Ensemble rather led the way at that time with a new freedom of musical expression – a movement that became known as Gnaffism. Sadly, due to our diverse living arrangements ranging from Essex to

Bram and Paul brainstorming ideas.

Russell and Chris trying to take it all seriously.

Glasgow via Vancouver, we don't perform so frequently now. However, we live in hope of a grand reunion before we become totally incapable.

A selection of Gnaff Ensemble concert handbills (1982–1983)

10 – The London Symphony Orchestra

Early in 1981, an opportunity arose to work with the London Symphony Orchestra. The then 'fixer' was a lovely man by the name of John Duffy, formally a double bass player in the orchestra. He had the most remarkable memory of anyone I've met in his position, with everything totally under control. He would be walking down a backstage corridor and fire off random comments to people about concerts or recordings that involved them – showing complete mastery of his job.

The orchestra had some recording sessions coming up for a new film called *Lion of the Desert,* with music composed and conducted by Maurice Jarre (father of Jean-Michel Jarre of *Oxygène* fame). We used to joke that a whiff of sand and Jarre would be there – *Lion of the Desert, Doctor Zhivago, Lawrence of Arabia.* Much to the appreciation of my keyboard colleagues, the composer was also fond of multiple pianos – each with two players. I'm sure you will be well acquainted with the film *Mad Max Beyond Thunderdome,* another film with its fair share of sand. I believe that for this score Jarre used twelve pianists on six pianos. *Lion of the Desert* was very modest – just four pianos with eight players. Personally, I feel that once you have three or four pianos there's not much to be gained by adding more, but hey, who am I to say, and business is business! It seems that for this particular film the orchestra couldn't find an eighth player on their regular list who was free for all the days, so someone suggested giving me a call. On those sessions I was to meet some of the big names of the orchestral keyboard world at that time; Michael Reeves, Leslie Pearson, Vivian Troon, Michael Round, Robert Noble, Richard Nunn and Martin Goldstein.

I must have done something right, as from then on the phone started to ring quite regularly from the LSO to the point that from the mid-eighties, I spent a great deal of time with the orchestra either at the Barbican Centre, in a studio or on tour. I got on very well with the LSO's pianist, Robert Noble. Bob had been the orchestra's longest-serving third horn player from 1955–1970 and subsequently sixth, utility horn from 1970–1984. He was also a fine pianist, and when he eventually stepped down from his third horn position, he also became the orchestra's pianist

Drinks with Robert Noble in Brussels (late '80s)

when required. I greatly valued the company of this somewhat private person; his quiet, dry humour, not to mention the pints of lager. It was a privilege at that stage in my career to sit next to him for works like Stravinsky's *Petrushka* – playing the minor celeste part but also absorbing the practicalities and geography of the challenging solo piano part, which I would subsequently play many times myself. Sadly we lost Bob in February 1992 when he passed away at the start of a recording session at Abbey Road Studios for Ives' *Three Places in New England*. This was a truly shocking afternoon when we were all in a state of disbelief. The sessions were reorganised shortly afterwards at Watford Town Hall, and the recording is dedicated to Bob's memory. I'm delighted to still be in touch with his widow, Maire.

During this time, I had the opportunity to work with some of the world's most eminent conductors. Claudio Abbado was still very much in evidence, also Seiji Ozawa, Rafael Frühbeck de Burgos, Sir Colin Davis, Michael Tilson Thomas and, of course, Leonard Bernstein. I sat behind Abbado once for an LSO concert featuring Peter Schickele and the music of P.D.Q. Bach – he was in hysterics, as indeed he was meant to be! Playing under Abbado was exciting. However, he nearly always conducted from memory, which could bring challenges, especially for music such as Bartók's *The Miraculous Mandarin* when he lost his place!

I worked with Leonard Bernstein in 1986 for performances of his Second Symphony, *The Age of Anxiety* – a programme which also included his *Chichester Psalms*. This was the final concert of the Bernstein Festival. This symphony is a piano concerto in all but name and the soloist was Krystian Zimerman. The work also has a very prominent celeste part that needs a large compass – five octaves. Unfortunately, the celeste supplied for the first rehearsal was only four octaves. The moment came for the four solo low E flat celeste notes, and I had no choice but to play them an octave higher. The rehearsal stopped, and I explained that another instrument was on its way. During the break a replacement celeste arrived, but although it had five octaves, it was the wrong five octaves, stopping (unusually) short of the required low E flat – I was now starting to panic. Inevitably Bernstein went back to cover the troublesome passage before I'd been able to warn him about the new situation. Again the rehearsal stopped and the maestro, still preserving his cool, asked, "Hey, what's the problem now?" I explained that we now had a new instrument, but with the wrong five octaves – he rolled his eyes and carried on. We did eventually get the right instrument, and I remember a small smile from the maestro when we next played that passage.

The following day we were rehearsing next door in the Guildhall School of Music and Drama, and during the morning break Bernstein came over to chat to me – I have to admit to this creating a degree of 'anxiety'. In fact, he did all the talking – not about having the wrong instrument but to explain the significance of the celeste part and this particular section of the work called *The Mask*. Towards the end of the final rehearsal, my colleague, who was playing the orchestral piano part (including a short solo passage), had decided that as we were close to 1:00pm, Bernstein would not go back to earlier in the work and somewhat uncharacteristically, went home. At this point I started to feel a little uncomfortable and, of course, the inevitable happened – being oblivious to any traditions of time or financial constraints, Bernstein decided to run the symphony right through from top to bottom.

This caused a degree of apoplexy with the management, but people like Bernstein were not used to people saying 'no'. It would be fair to say that this decision put me in a state of mild terror. For the whole run-through I was waiting for the moment when I might be able to dash from the celeste to cover the piano solo with barely a bar to get there. Some might say that I should have noticed the chunky TV cable lying across the stage floor, but in that moment of heightened excitement I must have lost my presence of mind and suddenly found myself lying on the floor – the rehearsal stopped yet again. This is it, I thought...

"Hey, what's going on? Where's the other guy?" he called over – more with frustration than annoyance. I simply said that he'd been taken unwell. "Not your day is it?" he said.

Also involved in that concert was Aled Jones, who was singing the treble solo in the second movement of Bernstein's *Chichester Psalms* – an exquisite setting of the twenty-third psalm and beautifully sung. Many years later we worked together regularly when he was presenting *Friday Night is Music Night* and we had great fun. We still manage the occasional catch-up, frequently for Christmas concerts, and most recently we enjoyed ourselves in such a show at the Barbican Centre, when we proved that Aled can still sing the opening of 'Walking in the Air', as he used to! A lovely chap with a great sense of humour who has achieved great things – one of them being the national speed record for getting from the stage at the end of a *Friday Night* to the stage door! Aled joined us for a repeat performance of the Bernstein programme in the Accademia Nazionale di Santa Cecilia in Rome. This was particularly memorable in that the whole orchestra was on stage after the interval ready to play the symphony, but

Bernstein's *Chichester Psalms* • Aled Jones with Leonard Bernstein and the LSO at the Barbican (May 1986)

the maestro was apparently not joining us. We all sat waiting on stage for a very long time, I would estimate some fifteen minutes, and slow hand-clapping had started before Bernstein eventually appeared. I have no idea what that delay was about, but I know that for the most part the orchestra was on autopilot for the symphony.

One fun anecdote that perfectly highlights the thinking of some illustrious maestros occurred during rehearsal. Bernstein spent most rehearsals sitting on a stool on the podium with his trademark white cigarette holder in his left hand, conducting with his right. On one occasion, a young lady member of the security staff was volunteered to tell him that smoking wasn't allowed in the hall. He allowed her to stand for some considerable time before he deigned to acknowledge her presence. "Yeah?" he said in mild irritation. "Excuse me, maestro, but the cigarette," she said. "Hey, is it troubling you?" And with that, he moved the cigarette to his right hand and continued to beat with his left. The girl left the stage forlorn and in defeat.

Also very much involved in that 1986 Bernstein Festival with the LSO was Bramwell Tovey, who stood in at the very last moment to replace the indisposed Lucas Foss for the opening concert. The concert was a triumph – the great man invited Bram to masterclasses in his Tanglewood Music Festival, and this whole event proved to be a career-changing moment.

This was a golden period for music in the UK. The CD format had not long been established, and orchestras were rerecording much of the standard repertoire. The LSO had also embarked on what was to be a long and fruitful relationship with the Chandos label and the conductor Richard Hickox. I enjoyed a very happy friendship with Richard, who delighted in calling me "stupid boy" when, sitting at a remote organ console and, out of earshot, I had failed to hear a vital instruction! He was very loyal to me and invariably asked for me if there was any question of a conflict of booking, such as when we came to perform and record Britten's *War Requiem*. There was talk of the boys from St Paul's Cathedral coming with their own chamber-organ player as, in this work, they are a self-contained, offstage unit. Richard stepped in and said that he wanted me there – such a kind gesture. In fact, by doing so, I got to spend time with the director of music at St Paul's, the illustrious John Scott who, like Richard Hickox, passed away well before his time.

To digress briefly – the first time I met Richard Hickox might well have been my last. We were in Lincoln Cathedral in the early eighties for a performance of Fauré's Requiem. For reasons we never established, the promised chamber organ didn't materialise, and I had no option but to play this somewhat intricate part on the main cathedral organ up on the choir screen. The rest of the assembled company were way below – the BBC Singers and beyond them, the BBCCO. Furthest away from me, and next to Richard Hickox, was the soprano soloist for whom I had to accompany the *Pie Jesu*. Straightaway I realised this would be problematic, and Radio 3 kindly arranged for a foldback speaker in the organ loft with a feed from the soprano's microphone. Unfortunately, due to the distances involved, and the nature of the gentle organ sound, Richard and the soloist were hearing the organ quite late, and he was getting understandably concerned. It took some reassurance from the production crew that the sound for the broadcast was absolutely spot on. He was also concerned about the sound in the cathedral being late for the audience, but there was no easy fix that would leave everyone happy, and it was a very uncomfortable situation. In the event it worked out well, as did the recording, but it was all quite nerve-racking – probably the only time that I've ever wanted to leave a situation and say "this isn't for me"!

It was a few years later when Richard and I crossed paths again, and the occasion was the LSO's first major choral recording for Chandos – Elgar's *The Dream of Gerontius,* which was made in the old Watford Town Hall (now the Colosseum). This was the first of a lengthy series of pioneering recordings to be made for Brian and Ralph Couzens of Chandos with the LSO and Richard. After that, most recordings took place at St Jude's Church, Hampstead Garden Suburb, where we recorded a large number of albums, including Mendelssohn's *Elijah* and the other major oratorios of Elgar – *The Kingdom* and *The Apostles.* These were great musical and social occasions, as the whole of the London Symphony Chorus was also involved and breaks frequently became large-scale picnics!

Most of these recordings would, quite sensibly, follow rehearsals and a performance in the Barbican Hall, which made for much smoother progress with the subsequent recording, as the repertoire was already very familiar. My parents would usually come to these choral concerts, and on many occasions my good friends Jonathan and Deborah Venner would also attend – happy times.

The recording of the Brahms' Requiem was memorable for the number of organs that passed through my hands and feet. It was decided early on that the pipe organ in the church was too unreliable and asthmatic, with lots of escaping wind – not good for quiet recording conditions. Chandos therefore hired in an electronic for the occasion. Unfortunately, whilst recording, the electronic organ would turn itself off without warning. A replacement organ was brought in, and the same thing happened. On the third occasion that this occurred, and knowing that we were heading towards the substantial C major chord in the sixth movement, I decided to take action and went and opened up the pipe organ. All was well, and any prevailing wind noise from the bellows was drowned out by the assembled company!

Various other recordings were made in St Jude's at that time, including an album of music by John Ireland with his setting of *Vexilla Regis* and its splendid organ part. There were also recordings of Vaughan Williams' symphonies with Bryden (Jack) Thomson, which included the monumental *Sinfonia Antartica*. In retrospect, I really wish that I had been able to use the church organ for the big solo in that work.

Possibly the most remarkable recording we made in this period was Britten's *War Requiem*. St Jude's was packed from end to end – the chorus at the west end, then the main orchestra and Richard. Behind him was the chamber orchestra and in the choir area were the boys from St Paul's Cathedral with their director John Scott, and me playing the chamber organ. I think I also slipped in the big organ chord in the *Libera Me*, which usually needs a second player, but not in recording as there are no logistical considerations. Part way through the recording, Philip Langridge, who was singing the solo tenor part, lost his voice. It was decided to carry on without him, and by means of expert timing and preparation, Philip later overdubbed (added) the missing sections of the tenor part to what had already been recorded – quite a feat. Incidentally, Philip gave the most moving eulogy at Richard Hickox's memorial service in St Paul's Cathedral – I think it may still be available on the internet.

It was unfortunate that certain residents close to St Jude's took exception to these large-scale recordings, and for quite a while an embargo was put on the numbers that could be involved in such projects. The consequence of this being that many subsequent recordings were moved south to All Saint's Church in Tooting. These included the later recordings of the ongoing Elgar project – *The Light of Life, The Black Knight* and *Caractacus*.

The mid-eighties were also highly productive years for the recording of film soundtracks, with many American production companies keen to come to the UK to record music soundtracks for their films. A regular visitor was the late James Horner, an American who had moved to London to study at the RCM. The first film I worked on with him was *Aliens*. As for most of his scores, there were two pianos and Bob Noble would play piano one. My part seemed to involve me spending more time inside the piano than out, hitting the strings with a metal bar! Many of James' scores 'borrowed' from either his own works or those of established classical composers

Carmina Burana with Robert Noble, Michael Round (not seen) on celeste (Rouen)

(such as Schumann's Third *Rhenish* Symphony transmuted from 3/4 into a 4/4 march for the film *Willow*) – we had great fun keeping up with where the music was coming from! Some of James' scores were huge, with the instrumentalists and singers totally filling Abbey Road Studio 1. These were long but fun days, and sometimes we would spend a week or two at a time, recording for three sessions most days (10:00–13:00, 14:00–17:00 and 18:00–21:00). Challenging but rewarding. The pianos were invariably placed on the far side of the studio behind the violin sections and very close to the legendary horn section led by the great Hugh Seenan. I think this studio time spent with the LSO had a significant influence on my great love of, and writing for, the horn.

I hadn't seen James for some years, but a few years ago our plumber happened to mention doing some work for an American composer who had a flat in Covent Garden and whom he thought worked in films. As a stab in the dark, I asked whether his name was James Horner and he said yes. We were going to set up a meeting, but not long after the initial contact, James tragically lost his life in an accident whilst pursuing his passion for flying small planes.

The year 1985 had been exciting and productive; I had been busy preparing and recording my album of organ music by Percy Whitlock, I had been on a film set with one of Charlie's Angels, and I had watched Patrick Moore be dragged offstage by a floor polisher (more about that later). However, nothing had prepared me for the excitement of being onstage with the esteemed Jessye Norman, with whom I was lucky to share several performances, together with the LSO. It's not often that you sit on stage prior to a performance, with that sense of electric anticipation in the air before such an artiste walks on stage – this was always present when this amazing lady was about to make her entrance. The first occasion was for a performance of Mahler's Second Symphony (April 1985) when Jessye Norman was singing alongside the soprano Lucia Popp – an exquisite partnership. This was part of the orchestra's Mahler, Vienna and the 20th Century Festival with Claudio Abbado at the RFH. In September of that year, she performed Berg's *Altenberg Lieder,* for which I was playing the harmonium. I may be chastised for saying that this is, for me, not the most approachable music – however, I loved every minute of this experience! I was also involved in performances with her some years later at the Barbican Centre. These were notable for the rebuilding of the backstage area – moving the artist's bar (at that time in the area immediately behind the stage) up a floor and also putting large wooden screens around the area outside her dressing room!

That year also saw one of a number of short foreign trips around that time – one of which sticks firmly in the memory. We had flown into what was then East Berlin to give a concert that included the complete Stravinsky ballet *The Firebird* in the second half. Being at something of a loose end in the first half, I joined the percussion section for a brief stroll around the locality. We were dressed in our tails (which may have proven to be a fortuitous decision). Once we were a street or so away from the hall we seemed to be in a totally deserted part of the city. We continued walking, and after making a turn, we realised that we were looking straight at the Berlin Wall. Ben Hoffnung was particularly keen to take a closer look and hopped over the perimeter wire to get closer. All of a sudden, from nowhere, came three armed policemen whose job, no doubt, was to thwart any attempt to approach the mighty wall by anyone desperate to escape the concert. One officer immediately demanded, *"Papiere!"*

That may have been the moment when panic set in! We clearly didn't have any appropriate documentation, and although we tried to explain our predicament, they insisted we follow them. Now, this was not an ideal situation – we were in communist East Berlin being led away by armed police, and we were due on stage in around fifteen minutes – to say we were confident of our position might be misleading. It was clear that disobeying these gentlemen was not an option and, on the assumption that we were not going to be shot, at least not yet, the least that would happen is that we would be taken to the police station. We were marshalled along a couple of roads only to find ourselves back at the hall. Clearly the guards had worked out who we were and wanted to teach us a lesson. They suggested quite firmly that we didn't wander off again!

Later, after the concert, some of us, still dressed in our tails from the post-concert reception, headed to a nightclub for drinks, receiving some very strange looks. In retrospect, I'm rather surprised that more interest wasn't taken in our nocturnal activities; there again, perhaps it was ... We then visited the famous Brandenburg Gate, which stood symbolically as an impasse between East and West. The next morning we flew out of Schönefeld Airport and saw the grotesqueness of the wall for the first time. The Berlin Wall was destroyed in 1989 and an abiding memory of that time was Mstislav Rostropovich giving an impromptu concert by the wall, playing the Cello Suites by J.S. Bach – just two days later ...

So, perhaps a little sightseeing? (1985)

With Russell Jordan, Ben Hoffnung and Nigel Charman at the Brandenburg Gate (1985)

11 – Slava

It was in the late eighties that I received a phone call from the LSO to ask whether I would be prepared to meet with the eminent cellist Mstislav Rostropovich (Slava) to run through a concerto (Dutilleux) with him. This was a seminal moment in my career, and I was to spend a great deal of time over the next few years working with this great man, both in private rehearsal and also in recital. At that time Slava was making regular appearances as a conductor with the LSO, although he directed more through his innate musicianship and enthusiasm than basic technique. When we first worked together his London base was a converted school off the Holloway Road in north London – a lovely apartment but in a rather surprising location. As we finished our second day of rehearsal, he asked me the best way to get to the Savoy, where he was meeting a friend. My mind raced through the options – it was late evening and directing him via some dingy side road to the local Holloway Road Piccadilly Line station and the subsequent line changes to reach the Strand seemed inappropriate, so I put him in my car and drove him!

Slava had a history of commissioning new works to play and did a huge amount to develop the repertoire for his instrument. Some of the concertos would end up on my piano to learn and ultimately work on together in preparation for a performance with orchestra. Slava's command of English was good, but some subtleties continued to elude him – he would regularly say, "You tell me if I make sh*t." – i.e. mess up! It was after one particular rehearsal that I came to understand a little why musicians have such exorbitant insurance premiums – far higher than most professions. We were rehearsing in Slava's apartment, along with the conductor, Michael Tilson Thomas. When we had finished, they both got in my car, and I drove the three of us to the Barbican. Had we had an accident, the damage claims would have been formidable, especially when you also consider the cello that was on board.

I also spent time at Slava's home in Aldeburgh, where we would rehearse, chat and drink an extraordinary strawberry infusion that he liked to call tea. We strolled around the town – Slava wearing his cap – sometimes eating fish and chips from a newspaper. Somehow it seemed incongruous seeing him like this, compared to the man the world usually saw. Meanwhile, I would try to explain to him some of the antics that my friends and I got up to in Aldeburgh in former years!

On the occasion of my last visit, we had been invited to a lunchtime reception being organised in a house further along his road. This was attended by students from the Britten-Pears Foundation, and Slava was in his element, holding court with the young people who, of course, were hanging on to his every word. There was a potentially dangerous moment when Slava suggested we organise a party for the students later that evening in his home. However, this was thwarted by a phone call from the LSO with a schedule change, meaning that we would no longer be staying overnight in Aldeburgh.

Following further rehearsal in the afternoon, Slava stowed himself and his cello in my car for the drive back to London, though not before telling me how much his Stradivarius cello was insured for and what it was actually worth! We set off down the A12, but by the time we reached Gants Hill (by coincidence, my home at the time) Slava decided we should eat. This was a lucky place to get hungry as I clearly knew the local restaurants, and I have to admit to a smile at the memory of launching ourselves into the Mandarin Palace Chinese restaurant by Gants Hill roundabout. The first issue arose when we were barely inside the door – the restaurant was busy, and the manageress clearly wanted us to occupy a table for two. She therefore set about trying to wrestle Slava's cello from him to put in the cloakroom behind the front door. The cello won that battle, but then another problem arose – Slava was on a roll with gin and tonics. Not ordinarily a problem, but I was aware that I still had to drive him back to Holloway and then get myself back home. I tried to explain this to Slava, but he wasn't concerned, telling me that the following day he was having dinner with the Lord Mayor and if I had a problem, he would fix it ... Swift action was needed and after the second round of drinks arrived, I excused myself and, when out of sight, asked the manageress to put just water in my glass when more gins were ordered.

We had some fascinating chats, particularly about the time in August 1991, following the deposition of Mikhail Gorbachev, when Slava smuggled himself into Russia via Tokyo and into the Parliament Building in Moscow. It was quite extraordinary to hear him talking at first hand about his telephone call from Boris Yeltsin, telling Slava that he wished him no harm, but he did plan to storm the building and if he remained there, his safety couldn't be guaranteed.

One particularly memorable recital in the late eighties involved us boarding the Hennessy private jet at Gatwick and flying down to Cognac in south-western France – the only time I've ever taken off sideways! We were due to play a recital for the retiring chairman of Hennessy cognac, to be followed by a substantial banquet. As it turned out, the recital proved to be the least of the day's challenges.

Shortly after taking off, we started to descend. I asked Slava why we were landing so soon, and he told me that we had to pick someone up. We landed at Paris-Le Bourget and there on the tarmac was the renowned conductor, Seiji Ozawa. He and Slava were great friends and, as it turned out, at the time he was music director of Hennessy Opera in Tokyo. Pleasantries out of the way, we carried on to land at what passed for an airport at Cognac, with no passport formalities, of course, and a waiting limousine to take us to the Hennessy chateau.

My first problem was discovering that with our schedule that day being brought forward by a couple of hours, I had packed too hastily and forgotten a white shirt before rushing to meet Slava in his new

Recital with Slava and celebrity page-turner, Seiji Ozawa, Cognac (late '80s)

London base in Little Venice. Luckily that carelessness was easily fixed by our host. The next issue was not so fixable – Slava had asked Seiji to be my page-turner!

If that suggestion wasn't enough, Slava had developed a little pantomime whereby at the start of our performance he would be 'offstage' with his cello and Seiji. Apparently I was to address the audience in French and explain that they were to be entertained by a world-famous cellist for whom I would be playing the piano. I was growing more uncomfortable by the second … I don't frequently address French people in their *'langue naturelle'*, but it seemed that I didn't have much say in the matter. At this point I thought it sensible to take advice and write something down.

Slava's plan was that, following my speech, Seiji would walk in with the cello and start to tune, which would obviously not end well. There would then be some failed attempts to make music to a highly confused audience and eventually call for help from his friend. This all went pretty much to plan, although I can't guarantee what the assembled company might have made of my attempt to massacre their language. The pantomime over, I felt relatively confident that the performance aspect would not present the same mind-focusing considerations. However … I saw another dilemma rapidly unfolding, as it appeared that Seiji (who had not come in for our rehearsal) didn't intend to stand up to turn my pages. Those who know him will know that he is somewhat vertically challenged, and if you know the Scherzo from Shostakovich's Sonata for Cello and Piano, you will also be aware that it contains a very sudden and sharp leap for the left hand to the bottom of the piano, coincident with a page-turn. As things stood, I was very likely to make powerful and unexpected contact with my distinguished page-turner's right arm. When the moment came, I remember muttering 'sorry' to Seiji as I whacked his arm forcefully, causing him to withdraw it swiftly from the field of battle. He didn't seem unduly phased by this or make any attempt to stand up for later repetitions. It was a privilege to play works such as the Shostakovich Sonata with Slava when, through his friendship with the composer, he had such a personal understanding and connection with the music.

Slava had extraordinary stamina and seemed to thrive on both playing and socialising to the maximum. He would regularly catnap and excuse himself to do so if we were making a car journey. On one occasion we had a late evening rehearsal together in the Green Room of the Barbican, following a concert. After half an hour or so there was a knock on the door, and two rather glamorous young ladies greeted us. They were from New York and knew Slava from his time in the US – both were immediately welcomed into our midst. Slava went outside to talk to the security staff, after which we continued to rehearse with our new audience.

Some thirty minutes later there was a knock on the door and in came a platter of smoked salmon sandwiches, a bottle of vodka and four glasses – apparently our rehearsal was over! Slava was clearly set on a full-scale catch-up with his friends, and I was about to miss my last train. He insisted that I enjoy a little more hospitality, then he arranged for his driver

to take me home whilst he continued to party with the vodka and young ladies. When I saw him the next morning, I asked if he'd had a good time after I left. His reply, with a characteristic twinkle in his eye, "It is a cross I have to bear!" Whilst in Moscow for an RPO concert in 2013, I was touched that his daughter, Elena, sought me out in order to say hello – some years after Slava's passing, of course.

This was a very precious time in my life, and I will always feel the richer for having spent so much time with this generous and warm-hearted man.

With Mstislav Rostropovich and Seiji Ozawa, Cognac (c. 1990)

12 – The London Philharmonic Orchestra

Early in 1992 I received a call from John Cobb, previously a trombone player but by then, the 'fixer' of the London Philharmonic (I don't remember whether they were the London Philharmonic or the London Philharmonic Orchestra at the time – there seemed to be a period of indecision). The orchestra needed to replace the pianist for two performances of Stravinsky's *Petrushka* with the revered Klaus Tennstedt at the helm. There were two big considerations to this exciting prospect – firstly I was due to leave for the USA and Japan with the LSO before the second concert in Basingstoke. The second was Tennstedt's personal conducting style and its potential impact on surviving the piano part!

The first problem was luckily resolved by a phone call to the LSO office – I was told that I wasn't needed for the first two days in New York and there were apparently two others also flying out late. They would therefore arrange for us to all travel together after the main group. Orchestras are sometimes happy to make such arrangements if flights can be changed. They also potentially save on travel, concert and hotel fees for the days you're not there. For the second issue I would have to put my trust in the maestro. In practice, it couldn't have been more straightforward. Tennstedt's innate musicianship and sense of rhythm somehow conveyed every nuance. There wasn't a moment's indecision, and he was very generous to me throughout. I'm delighted to have discovered that the RFH performance has now been released on CD although I believe that, strangely, the pianist is anonymous!

Two short postscripts to that story – while I was waiting at Heathrow for my flight to New York and reading my guide book to Tokyo (the second leg of our tour) a young lady greeted me enthusiastically and asked if I was going to Tokyo. I explained that I wouldn't be there for another week. Her name was Mandy Dumbleton (now Ureña), she worked in Tokyo, and

With Jo, our friend Rebecca from New York, Mandy and husband, Orlando, New York (2005)

she would be delighted to show me around. This is what happened, and we remain friends to this day, although she is no longer based in Tokyo.

Having met up with my co-travellers, the three of us arrived in New York. The weather was atrocious, and this being our first time in the city, we were unaware of the unconventional traditions of the private taxi operators! We succumbed to one particular gentleman who quoted us $50 to the city centre – reasonable, we thought, and in we got. When we arrived at our hotel in Times Square he had managed to add on some $60 for tunnels and tolls – the bill was more than double. He was adamant that he had said $50 plus tolls. Maybe he did, maybe he didn't, but be warned! Luckily the LSO was sympathetic in its reimbursement. At least we weren't driven down a back street and forced to hand over all our money, as happened to a good friend of mine.

I only worked with Klaus Tennstedt three times – *Petrushka* being the last. The first was for a performance of Carl Orff's *Catulli Carmina* – part of a trilogy that includes *Carmina Burana*, a work I've performed more often than may have been good for me, but it does have a certain excitement. Having three keyboard parts (two pianos and celeste), it does occasionally afford the opportunity for my wife Jo to join me. *Catulli Carmina* is a curious work but notable for keeping four pianists (on four pianos) gainfully employed. The lengthy central *a cappella* section is challenging for the chorus, and Richard Cooke (then chorus master of the London Philharmonic Choir) had been at pains to caution

Klaus Tennstedt • Mahler's 'Eighth' at the RFH (Jan. 1991)

the LPO that there was really not enough preparation time, as this was non-standard repertoire. During the Festival Hall rehearsals there were at least two hastily gathered board meetings onstage because the maestro wanted to cancel the performance. However, in the event, everyone rose to the occasion, as is so often the case in our profession, whether hampered by lack of rehearsal, poorly printed or illegible parts or incompetent direction.

LPO and choruses • Klaus Tennstedt • Mahler's Eighth Symphony at the RFH (January 1991)

The second occasion was for three performances early in 1991 of Mahler's *Symphony of a Thousand*. Due to the forces involved, this work doesn't come up frequently for reasons of space and cost, which is why I have kept a tally of performances. At the time of writing, I have just completed performance number seventeen, with the CBSO in Birmingham.

The downside of the LPO performance, if it could be described as such, was that it was held in the Royal Festival Hall, which is perhaps too small for this piece – the massed choirs wrapped right around the stage and out onto the side terraces. It was a particular pleasure to meet up again with some good friends from the London Symphony Chorus such as Hilary Matthews, Maggie Donnelly and Hugh Alford – we had spent so much time together in former years, and they were helping to bolster chorus numbers for this work. The performances were recorded and broadcast for BBC Two. This piece is very good socially, as there are four keyboard parts: organ, harmonium, piano and celeste. I've worked my way through all four parts over the years, although mostly I've played the spectacular organ part, with the harmonium coming a close second – which is what I played on this occasion. Although the piano, celeste and harmonium only play in Part II (a setting of the closing scenes of Goethe's *Faust*), we were asked to be on stage for the much shorter Part I (a setting of the Pentecostal hymn, 'veni creator spiritus') to maintain visual continuity for the TV recording. I have to say that this is the only time I can remember sitting on stage for twenty-five minutes, not playing a note, and being emotionally drained at the end! Such was the command of Klaus Tennstedt and his musical empathy with Mahler. If you can find the BBC recording or DVD, I urge you to watch it. The lighting is not what it would be today, and it won't have the same impact as being in the hall, but it's very impressive. Just turn up the volume and treat the neighbours!

Roderick Elms *harmonium*, Michael Round *celeste*, Richard Nunn *piano*, James Ellis *mandolin* and Malcolm Hicks *organ*. Mahler *Symphony of a Thousand* (January 1991)

There should have been a fourth collaboration for me with Tennstedt for Haydn's *The Creation* (February 1993) but, as on so many other occasions latterly, he cancelled for health reasons. I had been booked to play the harpsichord, although I had suggested that this should really be a fortepiano – the forerunner of our modern piano. Apparently the maestro had disagreed, but this was not the reason for his cancellation! There followed a period of some uncertainty about who would conduct the performances. I was chatting with my good friend Frank Wilson, with whom I regularly joined to engage in my lifelong hobby of sound recording. A great Haydn aficionado, Frank had recently attended Sir Roger Norrington's *Haydn Experience* at London's South Bank and suggested he would be an ideal candidate for the job. I duly passed on this suggestion to the LPO office. I have no idea whether it was this suggestion or one from another route, but within a day or so Roger had been booked for the occasion. This was very good news, at least from my perspective, as he proved to be the most gifted 'teacher' you could wish for this work – the music was in his blood. I joined Roger on several occasions following *The Creation*, both with the LPO and elsewhere for piano rehearsals, and have always found him inspiring, highly personable and great company.

At the first rehearsal for *The Creation*, Roger suggested that I, along with the three soloists (Felicity Lott, Anthony Rolfe Johnson and David Wilson-Johnson) should go to the Green Room, together with the fortepiano, and work on some of the soloists' sections. I'd not previously played a fortepiano in this context, although I knew it to be the correct instrument. I therefore asked Roger whether he had any particular words of guidance as to what he would like from me. "Just come and go as you think fit – follow your instincts," he said, and that's what I did. He rather endearingly referred to me in a BBC interview for the broadcast as "The Jack Russell of the orchestra!"

There were many memorable performances with the LPO during this period, and these included my one experience of working with Sir Georg Solti, who had preceded Klaus Tennstedt as music director (1979–1983). It was interesting to hear colleagues talk about Solti, as there was a significant divergence of opinion – he was gravely unpopular with many orchestral musicians, though singers seemed to love him. He had become more irritable in later life and didn't always treat orchestral players respectfully.

The occasion was Handel's *Messiah*, which I approached with a degree of anxiety, having heard many of the stories about Solti and his manner. Simon Preston had been engaged to play harpsichord continuo, but someone from the LPO office felt that there should probably also be an organ. Solti was asked whether he also wanted an organ and his answer was that they should listen to his Chicago recording and arrange for whatever he did on that – it's always good to have someone in charge who knows his mind! In practice, he seemed to know the recitatives and arias in which he would like to hear the organ, and it was all very amicable. As expected, the singers were eating out of his hand, and it was also a pleasure to hear Simon's characteristically flamboyant harpsichord realisation!

Another memorable performance was of Messiaen's *Turangalîla-Symphonie* (March 1998). Once again at the orchestra's RFH home, the performance was conducted by Sir Mark Elder with Peter Donohoe doing the honours with the hugely challenging solo piano part and Cynthia Millar playing the ondes Martenot. I always really enjoyed working with Mark, both with orchestras and in piano rehearsals. I'm aware that some of my then colleagues found him a little earnest, but to my mind, this was a virtue. Like Sir Roger Norrington, his passion for the music and its interpretation was paramount.

Due to the orchestral excesses of this piece, there was an extra stage extension at the front, which was clearly not as substantial as the rest of the stage. I was sitting at the celeste, just in front of the conductor, and from time to time during some of Peter's more exuberant piano passages, the whole stage would move up and down in a most disturbing fashion.

This was a very exciting performance, after which I was delighted to be greeted backstage by my friend Kate Quarry, and her husband Paul. Kate was pregnant and told me her babies had shown great interest during the music. I subsequently discovered that she gave birth to twin girls some nine hours later and nine weeks prematurely – such enthusiasm for life!

I shared several performances with the revered Bernard Haitink, a musicians' conductor who, like Klaus Tennstedt, had 'served his time' sitting in an orchestra rather than just standing in front of one. On one occasion, as we had completed the final rehearsal of Prokofiev's Fifth Symphony, this great man slowly closed his score, turned to the orchestra and, as I remember, said, "Thank you for making my first experience of this work so memorable." There was a sense of amazement – you would have thought that he'd been conducting the piece all his life. Most of us have gaps in our repertoire, but you somehow don't imagine it of someone at this stage of their career. If I remember correctly, the orchestra broke into spontaneous applause.

A career highlight came with an invitation to record some piano concerto movements for CDs being produced by the American company Victoria's Secret. I'd always wanted to break into the lingerie market, and this was my opportunity! These were initially with the LSO and later the LPO. There were quite a few of these recordings over the years, but the last was unforgettable because, due to a misunderstanding, I wasn't actually engaged – at least, I was booked for the recording session but no mention made of any solo recording. I turned up at the much-lamented CTS Studios nestled in the shadow of Wembley Stadium and now demolished following the redevelopment. There was a piano at the front with its lid up, concerto style. There was also a celeste at the back of the studio with some music on it. I was told that they were recording the concerto first and so I went up to the canteen and ordered breakfast (CTS was famed for its breakfasts as well as its fridge-chilled KitKats). Halfway through my second rasher of bacon, the fixer, John Cobb, raced up to me and said, "Rod, they need you." I asked why, as I understood they were recording the concerto first."Yes," he said, "that's you!"

I remember giving the situation some consideration. There was the unfinished breakfast to consider, and the eggs were congealing in a not-so-endearing manner. Also, there was the matter of the music – the slow movement of Chopin's First Piano Concerto, which I'd never played. They were insistent that this had to be recorded now, and I remember being quite assertive and saying that they would have to rearrange the recording order. They would also need to find me a room with a piano to learn the piece and, if I felt comfortable and we agreed the usual fee, I would record it after the orchestral break – meanwhile I would finish my breakfast while all this was arranged. I think they realised that, in the circumstances, this was not at all unreasonable. I felt sorry to upset the record company's plans, but it turned out that as I had made their previous solo recordings, they had assumed that I would be there ready to record the Chopin – orchestras don't make such assumptions!

The orchestra also embarked upon a series of symphonic 'pop' albums with the likes of Procol Harem and Led Zeppelin. Probably my favourite recordings in a less-classical genre were two albums with the legendary composer Lalo Shifrin (of *Mission: Impossible* fame) whom we joined for two recordings of his music at CTS Studios – *Jazz Meets the Symphony* (2003) and *More Jazz Meets the Symphony* (2004). For these, the orchestra was joined by the legendary US jazz players Ray Brown (bass) and Grady Tate (drums) – both terrific albums.

There were some wonderful foreign tours with the LPO during the nineties. In 1993 we made the first trip by a British orchestra to South Africa in more than forty years, due to the constraints of apartheid, and we were treated like royalty. As this trip was confirmed fairly late in the day, the only flights that could be booked were mostly 'red-eye specials', so most days involved a rehearsal and concert with a reception afterwards, followed by a really early start. The upside of this being a little time to explore the next city during the morning. We started in Johannesburg, then visited Bloemfontein, Pretoria, Durban, Port Elizabeth, Cape Town and Sun City. Along the way we saw game reserves, spent time being entertained on a wine farm in Western Cape Province and, as there was an educational aspect to the trip, small groups of us played for children in townships outside Port Elizabeth and Soweto, which is the largest city in South Africa. Our final stop was Sun City – a somewhat diminutive Las Vegas. Everything was larger than life, and my particular

Alistair Young on the artificial beach, Sun City (July 1993)

Keith Millar has a little flutter, Sun City (July 1993)

hotel was located within a casino. Outdoors there were great attractions, including fake beaches, living museums, animal sanctuaries and a vast water park with probably the longest waterslide I've ever had the courage to go down. We toured with the then music director, Franz Welser-Möst and the programme included Shostakovich's First Symphony and Bartók's *Dance Suite*. For this, I was joined by my good friend and regular touring companion, Alistair Young. Also on the trip was a brilliant young percussionist, Graham Cole, who was sadly to leave us at a very young age not so long afterwards, and way before his time.

The giant water slide in Sun City (July 1993)

Whilst in South Africa, I experienced one of those amazing coincidences that can happen when abroad. Before leaving home, I had dropped a note to my conductor friend Clive Fairbairn and his wife Nicky, who were living at the time in Bophuthatswana, where he was artistic director of the orchestra of the Department for the Performing Arts Council. I had written to him to say that we were coming, but I knew that was a pretty futile gesture in view of his location. I tried to ring when we arrived, if only to say hello, but there was no answer. Leaving our rehearsal in the theatre in Cape Town later that week, we were tooted by a car from the pedestrian crossing ahead – Clive and Nicky, a thousand miles from their home!

There was another special meeting to come out of this particular tour. I arrived in Cape

Town knowing that my father had been stationed there with the RAF during the war. Before I left on tour, Dad had reminded me that he had had a friend there who had served in the South African Air Force, and I said I would try to track him down. Not holding out much hope, I started to make phone calls to numbers picked from the phone book. On my third attempt, I explained that I was hoping to find someone who had served with my father – there was a silence then, "That was my husband!" It turned out that this lady's husband had passed away in the previous year. However, she took Alistair and me on a tour around Cape Town, showing us some of the haunts they occupied during the war – all very special. It also turned out that a couple of years earlier, they had been to London with similar thoughts, but not managed to find my parents.

In 1994, I joined the orchestra for two performances of Percy Grainger's wacky *The Warriors*. The other two solo pianists on this occasion were Wayne Marshall and Penelope Thwaites. During a rehearsal break at the RFH, Wayne asked me about the famous RFH organ, which he had never played. As it was likely unlocked, I suggested he 'had a play'. He sat down and improvised, gently at first, for a good five minutes, working expertly through the organ as though they were old friends, building to full organ. By this time, many of the orchestra had returned from their break and were sitting in the hall, similarly fascinated by his impromptu performance.

For a while, the LPO ran a series of Sunday morning concerts for families, and in February 1997 I was invited to perform the celebrated Scherzo from the *Concerto Symphonique* No. 4 for Piano and Orchestra by Henry Litolff. I remember encountering this piece when I was eight, playing it as a piano-duet in a concert with

Grainger's *The Warriors* with Wayne Marshall and Penelope Thwaites, RFH (1994)

my first piano teacher, Freda Ellinger. The work has become something of a party piece, and this particular performance with the LPO was made particularly special due to the fact that my lifelong friend, Bramwell Tovey, was conducting. We were also joined in the audience at the Royal Festival Hall by our former mentor from Redbridge, Malcolm Bidgood, who I think was probably quite proud to see two former protégés together on the platform. On that occasion (and has frequently been the case) Bram acted as compère – something that he has always done with great aplomb and charisma. Those of us who grew up together are all delighted that, despite his heavy conducting schedule in North America, Bram now has more reason to return to the homeland with his appointment as principal conductor of the BBCCO.

I didn't work much with the LPO's next music director, Kurt Masur. By the time I first met him, I was very well aware of his reputation – his musicianship and his fiery temper. This was to be a piano rehearsal with the maestro and Sir Willard White for a concert in which he was performing some Gershwin songs. We were told that in a former life, Masur had been something of an aficionado of Gershwin ...

I approached the RFH Green Room with some considerable trepidation, only too aware of the intimacy of the situation with this potentially 'volatile' maestro. However, he was most courteous and Willard as charming as ever – we had met on previous occasions for piano rehearsals prior to choral recording projects and *Friday Nights*. It was all going very well until we embarked upon one particular arrangement and then a degree of chaos ensued. The arrangement provided was not what Willard was expecting. In fact, what he was expecting was pretty standard and, by good fortune, I had played it with the BBCCO a week or two earlier. For possibly the first time in his life, Kurt Masur appeared to be at a loss for words, mostly managing, "Vot iz to be done?" The solution, by way of a small cut, was really very simple. The question was, whether I had the confidence to show the maestro what he was missing. Somehow I found the necessary courage and tact, and Mr Masur was actually very gracious in accepting my suggestion. Willard treated me to a very good lunch!

The only other time I worked with Kurt Masur was for a performance of Brahms' Requiem in the RFH, for which I was playing the organ.

On this occasion the maestro had requested a professional choir rather than one of the London choruses, which I'm sure would have done a magnificent job. I don't remember the details, but Masur was extremely unpleasant to the choir, making everyone feel very uncomfortable. Kurt Masur was a formidable conductor but, like a handful of his colleagues, had a side to his character that frequently left performers feeling uneasy or even angry at his manner. A happy life on and off stage depends to a great extent on mutual respect between those present. You can generally judge that respect by the prevailing level of silence when the maestro walks on to start a rehearsal or recording.

Without a doubt, one of the most substantial and intensive projects of the late nineties/early noughties for the LPO was the recording of the music for *The Lord of the Rings* trilogy. The music was composed and conducted by the Canadian Howard Shore, now based in New York, and who became a good friend through these and earlier collaborations. *The Lord of the Rings* was a massive project and one that won Howard Academy, BAFTA, Golden Globe and Grammy Awards. Each year, over a period of some weeks, we would gather, mostly at Watford Colosseum, although for logistical reasons we had the occasional sessions at either Abbey Road Studio 1 or Air Lyndhurst Studios. Progress was steadfast, but the final result was remarkable. One or two 'stars' passed through along the journey, such as Sir James Galway to play the penny whistle, although much of this was ultimately played par excellence by Stewart McIlwham, the LPO's piccolo player. Some of my time would be spent inside the keyboard-end of the piano, making menacing sounds on the strings with a metal bar. On other occasions, the LPO's principal percussionist, Rachel Gledhill, could be found bending over the other end of the instrument, whacking the strings with copious amounts of black metal chain, much to the amusement of all concerned. However, contrary to general perception, this is a particularly specialised job, and Howard was visibly disappointed on one occasion when Rachel was not available to play.

On many occasions there would be an extended evening break so that Howard could share a video link-up with the director, Peter Jackson, in New Zealand to review some of the day's work. During most of these breaks I would go with my good friend Keith Millar and other percussionist colleagues to The Horns, next door, for dinner. On one occasion our meals arrived so late that we carried them back to the Colosseum and ate them backstage, between recordings!

It was a privilege to have shared in this landmark piece of cinema history, as well as part of the ensuing *The Hobbit*. One of the most personal sessions I experienced on this project was for the closing titles of *The Return of the King*, which were to include a song, sung by Annie Lennox. Annie actually studied flute, piano and harpsichord at the RAM and we overlapped for my last two years there, although, to my knowledge, we didn't meet at the time. I turned up at Abbey Road Studio 1 on something of a voyage of discovery to find it in near darkness apart from three black sofas, in a U-formation, some tungsten lamps giving a very dim and indirect light, and a piano at the open end of the 'U'. It turned out that she and I were to work through and develop musical ideas for the closing song, for which Howard joined us via a link from New York. It was a most fascinating afternoon and a pleasure to finally meet this lovely lady.

I played for several of Howard's film scores in the early nineties, and one particularly memorable one was *Ed Wood* (1994), featuring Johnny Depp. I spent an interesting morning in what is now The Music Studios

in Marylebone Lane, playing through Howard's sketches in the company of producer Tim Burton, who remained in his trademark black leather trench coat for the duration. The writing for this score was intriguing as Howard had a particular keyboard instrument in mind that we weren't able to source. We therefore assembled the most extensive collection of keyboard instrument options that I've ever seen in a studio, played by myself, Leslie Pearson

Leslie Pearson searching for that elusive sound • *Ed Wood* (1994)

and Vivian Troon. Following

the end of the last session, I stayed behind to try the effect of adding or subtracting various instruments and combinations of sounds. It became quite atmospheric being in the almost empty building at that hour – just the engineering crew in the control room with Tim Burton and Howard. Meanwhile, I was in the studio under the watchful eye of Tim's then fiancée, Lisa Marie, who had played the part of Vampira. It was well after midnight when we eventually called it a 'day'.

A final filmic mention should go to one other production that was released in 1996, *Looking for Richard* – a documentary view of Shakespeare's contemporary relevance through an analysis of *Richard III*. This had been directed and narrated by Al Pacino, who delighted everyone by turning up for one of the recording days at All Saint's Church, Tooting and deciding to play the bass drum with the orchestra, under the watchful eye of percussionists Rachel Gledhill and Andy Barclay. I was playing the lovely organ in Tooting, and I was touched to note that I received an on-screen credit for my efforts.

For this, and many other films over the years, the choral aspects would be contributed by London Voices with their director Terry Edwards and, more recently, with their co-director Ben Parry.

With Leslie Pearson and Vivian Troon working on *Ed Wood* at Air Lyndhurst Studios with the LPO and Howard Shore (1994)

13 – When Things Don't Go According to Plan

I've talked elsewhere about some of life's surprises, but I felt that Chapter 13 had to be exclusively about things that didn't go entirely according to plan or expectations – it's also the longest! I've been aware over the years that audiences can get quite excited when they notice that something has gone wrong. This can be unscheduled baton-tossing practice by the conductor (that happens more frequently than you might think) or something more subtle or even dramatic. Obviously, for the most part, we do our best to cover up small issues, but just occasionally, something more significant arises that is not so easily disguised.

One of the challenges of working in the Royal Festival Hall in former times was the stage layout that, when busy, meant that the piano was frequently set looking at the organ console rather than the conductor. That didn't usually seem to be of concern to the hall staff when they set the stage, and they would frequently tell me that no one else complained (which, of course, they did). This could pose a challenge for repertoire for which you needed a good view of the keyboard, the music and the conductor. There were occasions when we were so tightly packed that you couldn't sit comfortably, as the piano stool was jammed against the stage riser behind and you became something of a musical sardine. This came to a head one morning when I turned up to rehearse the piano part for Bartók's *The Miraculous Mandarin*. The stool was so far under the keyboard that I couldn't actually sit on it and was forced to play most of the quite tricky piano part kneeling on the stool, with Alistair Young (who was playing the celeste next to me) operating the pedal. Something had to be done for the future, so I suggested to the stage staff that they find an old piano stool and cut off one of the rear legs so that it could overhang the riser behind, giving a little more space in front of the piano. Although most were reluctant or just laughed, senior event manager Eddy Smith took me seriously and agreed that we should try it. It worked like a charm until the closure of the hall and the remodelling of the stage.

I've been fairly lucky so far as piano malfunctions are concerned. Of course, instruments vary enormously and are not always as you would want them to be. It's not uncommon to be confronted by a loud and brash piano, only to be chastised by a conductor for being too loud in some of the more hushed moments, even when using the soft pedal and barely tickling the keys. Many's the time that I've wanted to invite a conductor to come over and show me exactly how they would suggest I play it. Not something I've ever done, as I suspect I might have been in trouble. I usually express surprise, apologise, and promise to try harder!

I've only experienced two serious piano malfunctions; the first, not strictly the piano. I was in Ilford Town Hall to perform the Grieg Concerto, yet again. I walked on, sat down, and promptly ended up on the floor – a leg on the stool had come off. Not only that, but I also took the leader's music stand with me as I went. It was actually quite funny, very dramatic and no harm was done, and, of course, the audience loved it, once they had finished gasping and realised that all was well.

The other occasion could have been very serious. We were mid-rehearsal in Moscow (1st April 2013). The piano had been at the front of the stage for Stephen Hough to rehearse Saint–Saëns with the orchestra. The instrument was duly pushed back to my orchestral position, and I sat down. I had turned to the right and was talking to Alistair Young (*Fountains of Rome*, with celeste) when a leg came off the piano, resulting in a tonne of Steinway D crashing to the floor. Not surprisingly, this unexpected sonic intrusion stopped the rehearsal. On investigation, there had clearly been some previous repairs, and a leg had been reassembled with small one-inch screws. Moving the piano across the stage had simply pulled them out. I can't bear to imagine the consequences if I'd been sitting normally with my knees under the keyboard.

Perhaps just as memorable from that trip to Moscow, was the depth of

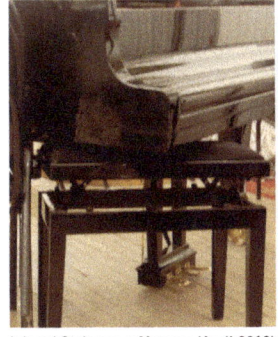 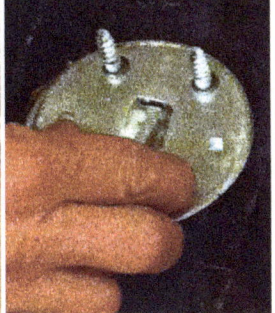

snow and the exceptionally low temperatures. Alistair and I spent a happy morning investigating Red Square, which was totally covered in a deep bed of white – a fairy tale, and so picturesque with the magic of St Basil's Cathedral at the

Injured Steinway • Moscow (April 2013)

far end. The only challenge of the visit was trying to take photos. Not wearing gloves was unrealistic and wearing them whilst taking photos, impractical!

So far I've been relatively lucky in respect of dress malfunctions and pretty much all I've had to cope with has been the lack of a white (or black) shirt. There was the unfortunate occasion when I was in Symphony Hall, Birmingham with the BBCCO for a live broadcast of *Friday Night* and due to play Saint-Saëns' *Wedding Cake* Caprice-Valse for Piano and Orchestra. A lively

St Basil's Cathedral, Red Square (April 2013)

and not-undemanding little number, but one that would undoubtedly necessitate standing up and facing the audience at the end. Due to lack of time, those in my eating party had decided to carry out a 'semi-pro' change of clothes – changing the shirt and trousers to save time later. We had decided to go to the local Indian restaurant, Shimla Pinks, in Broad Street. Apart from fine food, this restaurant had something of a reputation of under-the-counter 'extras' – not that we ever imbibed. However, on this occasion, the something extra came by way of a waiter dripping curry sauce down the front of my white dress shirt. There's not much to be done about curry stains, the shops were shut, and there were no spare shirts. Fortunately, a kind member of the backstage staff rallied to my rescue, whisking me upstairs to an office and painting out all the yellow stains with white Tippex. This quick-thinking colleague saved me from embarrassment but totally wrote off the shirt!

Men in the symphony orchestras have traditionally worn tails, and I think formal dress of some type is pretty much an expectation from audiences, as it certainly lifts an occasion and gives a unifying image. There is a growing trend to wear black open-necked shirts with black suits, and I admit to finding that quite attractive. It's less weight to wear, feels less fussy and makes travel and luggage arrangements more straightforward.

I mentioned earlier that in the mid-eighties, the BBCCO frequently organised gala concerts. For a while, these included the Radio 2 *Festival of Light Music*. The first of these I played in was at the Royal Festival Hall in 1985. A 'special' moment came in Malcolm Arnold's *A Grand Grand Overture*, which is scored for a large orchestra, including parts for organ, three vacuum cleaners, a floor polisher and rifles to finish off the miscreants. However, whereas in the rehearsal the stage lights had been on, in the performance everyone was having to rely on music stand lights – except for the poor organist, who had none. Just before my entry, the lights dimmed to a dark red, and the notes on my music pretty much disappeared from view. I somehow navigated this issue, but Patrick Moore, the eminent astronomer and musician, didn't fare so well. He was playing the floor polisher and, perhaps because he was also struggling with the lack of light, he managed to get the power cable caught around one of the rotating brushes and, with a sense of inevitability, he was dragged offstage by an ever-shortening power lead!

For the most part, I've done my best to keep my eyes open when working, but there was an embarrassing moment while rehearsing Strauss' *An Alpine Symphony* with the LSO at the Barbican. The organ doesn't enter until quite late into the work, but when it does, it's quite prominent. Perhaps ill-advisedly, on this occasion I had decided to sit out in the hall and enjoy some of the rehearsal. At this point, I made what might be considered an error of judgement, as I had clearly started to enjoy the music too much. There's an unnatural silence that occurs when a confrontation arises on stage, or something goes dramatically wrong – I opened my eyes to see the whole of the LSO and the conductor, Rafael Frühbeck de Burgos, looking at me. He spoke to me with his characteristic and somewhat nasal Spanish accent, "Would you like to join us?" I later apologised, but he actually seemed quite amused by the incident. I hope there are no other near-somnial moments that I have forgotten!

Christmas 1993 was memorable as I spent most of Christmas and Boxing Days practising! I had been asked by the LPO to record Frank Martin's Ballade for Piano and Orchestra as part of their ongoing series of recordings of Martin's music, with conductor Matthias Bamert and my friends at Chandos. Matthias had got to know Martin quite well when living in New York, clearly acquiring an empathy with his music. As the recording was at the very beginning of January, I was taking every opportunity of being prepared, and so I worked right over the festive period due to the lack of time immediately between Christmas and the recording. Doing my best to be organised, I had also made a visit to Steinway Hall in London to choose the instrument that I wanted to use and that felt most suitable for the music.

I arrived in good time for the recording at Goldsmiths College (now upgraded to a university), for what should have been more than one session. I had anticipated warming up on the piano, but there it wasn't ... apparently it was still on the van outside the hall, as they were unable to open the rear doors to unload it. In the event, another instrument had to be brought down from central London, taking a considerable amount of time and also rather negating my good intentions in selecting an appropriate instrument. We lost most of the afternoon and, in the event, we had barely one session to record the piece. Lady Luck was on our side, along with a great deal of goodwill from Matthias, the orchestra and Ralph Couzens of Chandos, and I believe this CD of Martin's complete ballades remains a recommended version. One aspect of this episode that always niggled is that Steinway never made any comment. They make the most wonderful pianos, but I felt they might have had the common courtesy to offer me an apology. The other individual ballades were recorded by Ian Bousfield, Celia Chambers, Peter Dixon, and Martin Robertson.

When a friend calls and asks whether you fancy a few days in Gran Canaria and also offers you a fee, what's not to like? The friend was the conductor, Adrian Leaper, formally co-principal horn of the Philharmonia Orchestra, after which he became assistant conductor of the Hallé Orchestra. At the time of this call (1991), he was director of the Orquesta Filarmónica de Gran Canaria. The flip side to a few days in the sun was that Adrian was about to give a performance of Stravinsky's *Petrushka* with his orchestra in Las Palmas and they had just found the solo piano part stuffed down the back of a radiator. What they couldn't find was the pianist, who had apparently fled in a degree of panic. This concert also included Mozart's Concerto for Flute and Harp, for which they were joined by the ebullient harpist Marisa Robles. We had a lovely time, and on the last day, I was introduced to the spectacular dunes in Maspalomas; a place I have

The dunes in Maspalomas, Gran Canaria (1991)

returned to with my wife on a couple of occasions for some winter sun.

There may have been something of a trend starting here, as I had a similar call from Adrian a couple of years later when he was due to be conducting a performance of Shostakovich's First Symphony with the Ulster Orchestra for Radio 3. This work has a relatively challenging piano part that needs significant cooperation from the conductor. I understand that, for reasons not divulged, they suddenly found themselves without the pianist who had been engaged. To my knowledge, Adrian has not subsequently found himself with an absentee pianist!

This particular Shostakovich symphony has a tricky moment where the pianist has a long chromatic scale from the top to the bottom of the piano within an *accelerando*. There is little opportunity for the pianist to watch the conductor, so you rely on their ability to work with you. Adrian was first class, unlike the young and naive conductor who turned up to conduct this work with the BBC. She started the rehearsal by asking me to play this passage alone so that she could hear how I played it. This makes absolutely no sense unless you're trying to freak out the pianist! When playing that passage, you judge your *accelerando* according to the context of what has gone before and what is about to happen – I explained that as tactfully as possible. There were no additional solos that day ...

I similarly remember a young French conductor asking to hear a celeste and flute passage alone before we had even rehearsed it with the orchestra. I said that I was happy to help, but as we'd not yet played this passage, I asked whether he could tell us what was wrong. He said that it's sometimes problematic, so he'd like to hear it alone. I suggested that we all play it together and address any problems should they arise – they didn't. Some passages are actually more difficult without the accompanying musicians and a sense of context and pulse. Why go looking for trouble? So frequently, orchestral musicians are treated without due credit for their professional experience, or as though they've never played the music in front of them, which they usually have. More often than not in such a situation, there's only one person on stage who has not previously performed the music ... it doesn't seem to occur to them that this might be the case!

There have been several other non-mechanical failures resulting in consequential problems. One afternoon I received a call from the 'fixer' of the London Concert Orchestra, Christian Rutherford. It appeared that for some unexplained reason, there was nobody sitting at the RFH organ for the rehearsal of that evening's performance of *The Glory of Christmas*. Shouldn't be too challenging without rehearsal, I thought. Likely the same programme as on many previous occasions – take the green and orange copies of *Carols for Choirs*, pop in a *Messiah* for good measure. What could go wrong? Well, that became apparent during the performance of 'O Holy Night' when it transpired that the orchestra was in the key of C and, somewhat embarrassingly, my part was in D flat. I'm indebted to my friend John Langley for reminding me of this incident and also for coming clean as being the librarian responsible for the faux pas!

It seems something of a miracle to me when you consider the complexity, and the number of moving parts in a pipe organ, that things don't go wrong more frequently. In all my years I've had three fairly impressive cyphers, as they are known – moments where the organ decides to take matters into its own hands and play itself, probably from innate boredom! The first occasion was during a Tchaikovsky evening in the Royal Albert Hall. Such evenings were, at the time, presented very frequently by the legendary impresario Victor Hochhauser. By chance, I turned on the organ during the interval to check that all was well and suddenly middle C, from the very loudest reed stop (the *Tuba Mirabilis*), decided to show off. It was agreed that I should climb up inside the instrument to locate the offending pipe. However, in doing so, I clearly needed to leave the organ turned on so as to identify the pipe. Climbing my way up through the organ, and gathering quite a bit of dust and fluff along the way, I could see out into the hall between the front pipes, and it was obvious that many people were becoming quite disturbed by the sound, which some of them apparently perceived to be a fire alarm. The pipe was removed before too much more anxiety was caused, but some ear defenders would have been welcome! I don't know how organ tuners cope with that situation for far longer than I had to endure it.

Without a doubt, my worst experience of a cypher was in July 1997 in Birmingham's Symphony Hall. The City of Birmingham Symphony Orchestra (CBSO) and Chorus, together with the visiting Cleveland Chorus from the US, had assembled for a big gala concert to celebrate EMI's centenary, to be conducted by Sir Simon Rattle. There had been an issue in the morning rehearsal, when the canopy above the stage had been lowered to facilitate the installation of microphones by Tony Faulkner. This being to record Nigel Kennedy's performance of the Elgar Violin Concerto. Unfortunately, the canopy had failed to go back up, and an engineer had to be brought up from London. Whilst this didn't disrupt the rehearsal of the violin concerto or the opening piece by Mark-Anthony Turnage, it completely negated rehearsing Walton's *Belshazzar's Feast*, due to the choirs and conductor being unable to see each other. Simon was quite philosophical and eventually decided that we should simply abandon the rehearsal, reconvening for the evening concert. We had rehearsed the previous evening, so it was not a cavalier decision!

View from inside the RAH organ looking through some of the Great pipework to the audience – prior to renovation.

This was well before the installation of the new Klais pipe organ, and I was using a hired electronic instrument. It was all going swimmingly, as you might expect, until we came to the closing bars of the Walton. There's a moment of total silence before the last orchestra entry, which is followed by an eclipsing, full organ chord. I had full organ drawn for this exciting moment, but right in the middle of the preceding silence, top F on the pedal organ sounded for all its worth. I immediately cancelled all the stops, but the damage was done. Never before, or since, have I wanted the ground to open up and to disappear. Afterwards, I went upstairs to explain to Simon, and he was very gracious and understanding about the whole incident; accepting that it was totally beyond my control – he knew something of organs and their strange habits! What really upset me was that some people were asking the orchestral management why they couldn't have got a 'proper' organist for such a prestigious occasion. I had performed and recorded that piece countless times, and that really was quite hurtful. Even the press reviewed the moment as "The high drama of an early organ entry". What is sad is that if any of these people had really known the piece, they would have realised that the final organ entry is a full chord and not a single note – the high F that sounded doesn't even figure in the final chord. I wrote to the two errant reviewers, who both replied to apologise but, of course, those apologies were never published.

The following day we assembled to record the work for EMI, and I was hugely grateful that Simon explained to everyone what had happened. However, what made me more than a little angry was the organ hirer turning up at the start of the recording to check that all was well. I told him what had happened, and he replied by saying, "Oh, it's done that before." I fear I was somewhat abrupt and told him that it shouldn't have happened a second time – he clearly had no concept of the implications of what happened, how it made me feel, and how it affected so many people. The recording is terrific, and I commend it to you for a listen.

My third incident occurred barely two weeks later during a Radio 2 Opera Gala concert from the RFH conducted by Robin Stapleton. I had turned on the organ during the interval, ready for the second piece of the half – Mascagni's Intermezzo from *Cavalleria Rusticana*. This time I was sitting to the side of the organ console for the first piece of the half, Rossini's *The Barber of Seville* Overture. Luckily so, because when a loud reed stop decided to sound a middle C sharp, there was no way I could be implicated. Although I immediately turned off the blower, there was still wind in the organ. By now, one of Rossini's famous crescendos was starting on its journey and helping to create a high sense of anticipation in the hall. Fairly soon the inevitable happened – the bellows finally expelled their last vestiges of wind, and the note fell to its death like a collapsing bagpipe. The result was electric: the hall erupted into spontaneous applause and cheering, all wonderfully broadcast live by Radio 2 with an appropriately cryptic appreciation from Ken Bruce at its conclusion.

I toured a good deal with the LSO back in the eighties and early nineties. It's curious to remember that the only three occasions for which I joined them outside of this country to play the organ, ended in a degree of comedy and not much played. The first was a trip in 1984 to Santander, for a performance of Mahler's Second Symphony with Rafael Frühbeck de Burgos. Concerts in the summer festival are held outdoors on a platform in the town square. No sooner had we arrived than I had a call in my room from the fixer, John Duffy, asking me to go down to the lobby as a young lady wanted me to go with her in a taxi – he had a slightly mischievous sense of humour. We ended up in the town music shop, and she asked me to decide which organ I wanted. Oh dear; all the options were small home-entertainment models of no practical use for the massive organ entry at the end of the work. I chose the one with the most fun-looking rhythm box, for no reason other than a way of making a decision! When it came to the rehearsal, the television wasn't working for the offstage brass players and, as I remember, I ended up helping them. I didn't play a note on the organ, which wouldn't have been heard anyway.

The second occasion was something of a marathon – the orchestra was already on tour in Italy, and I was due to join them for a performance of Brahms' Requiem in Perugia. This involved an epic journey, starting with a flight from Stansted to Rimini on an almost empty TriStar jet. There were around forty passengers on the plane so there was a good level of personal attention from the crew. Arriving in Rimini, I had to get a local train to Ravenna and then a bus into the mountains to the beautiful ancient town of Perugia. After checking into the hotel, I strolled along to the theatre for the rehearsal and did a double-take when I walked on stage ...

The Brahms organ part needs a good solid sound from the pedal department and, hopefully, something reasonably big for the manuals. What I was presented with was a single manual, three-stop continuo instrument with no pedals, best suited to the music of Bach and Handel. Lorin Maazel looked over before starting the rehearsal and asked to hear the organ; I gave a quick tootle on what was evidently never going to be the sort of sound required for this work – he rolled his eyes, said, "Right ..." in a slow drawl and moved on! Soon after that, the horn section, seated behind the organ, began to complain about the organ sound – the pipes producing a baroque 'chiff' which they found difficult to cope with. All this, combined with the lack of pedals and any sense of gravitas, led to my making a complete reappraisal of my position and deciding not to use the instrument. However, another significant aspect of my situation was that the concert was being televised, and in those days the TV fee was paid in cash after the performance at the side of the stage. I therefore worked my way through the entire Requiem, pulling out and pushing in varying combinations of the three available stops – all with the power chord for the organ unplugged! I have no idea whether Maazel was aware – probably not – but I'm sure that he would have been much happier that way than me trying to play along in a totally ineffectual way and upsetting the horn section.

The last 'failure' with the LSO was a visit to St David's Hall, Cardiff (I think that qualifies as another country) for extra recording sessions on Gilbert Kaplan's extravagant project to record Mahler's Second Symphony. Kaplan was a wealthy American businessman and an amateur conductor with a lifelong obsession for this symphony – he would travel the world to hear performances and discuss the work with the conductors. I was greeted in St David's Hall by the legendary recording engineer Tony Faulkner. "Hello Rod, what are you doing here?" This rather stopped me in my tracks – Tony is at the very top of his field and would have known only too well that there was organ at the end of the last movement, which is what we were due to record. It transpired that one of the reasons we were all in Cardiff was to rerecord the end of the symphony *without* the organ part, which was to be added in the States at a later date. Apparently, the LSO wasn't told this. What added to the joy was that I had given Christopher Thomas, a percussionist friend, a lift from his home in north London. Not a note was played, and I didn't leave early!

In September 1990, I was asked to play the organ for a thanksgiving service for the life of one of the LSO's great characters – violinist Sydney Colter. This was in St Giles Cripplegate Church, and with me in the organ loft was a string quintet from the orchestra. The piece selected for us to play before the service was the famous Adagio, generally attributed to Tomaso Albinoni, although his input was marginal compared with that of Remo Giazotto, who wrote most of it. This piece certainly does feature the organ, but by far the most mind-focusing part is the solo violin. Perhaps unwisely, although it didn't obviously affect proceedings, violinist Lennox Mackenzie took a peek over the organ gallery – sitting there below us were Mstislav Rostropovich and Michael Tilson Thomas!

Many friends know that since my late teens I have suffered from a severe cat allergy. This was occasionally problematic when arriving for dinner with hosts who hadn't mentioned their cat, or simply thought that if they put it out of the room there wouldn't be a problem – oh that it was so simple. One morning I set out to play for some soloists' auditions at a hall in central London. At the last minute, these were transferred to the London home of the maestro who was conducting the auditions. With no time to even consider the possibility of cats, I walked into his home and there they were. I tried to give due warning, but my words fell on deaf ears – this gentleman is not known for his understanding or concern for other people's plights, though he apparently has a great love of cats.

I imagine I lasted around thirty minutes – looking at my watch wasn't a priority; being totally fixated on trying to read the scores being presented through increasingly swollen eyes, inflamed as a result of the protein in the air from the cats' fur. By now, there was an almost continuous stream of sneezes to accompany the rather confused auditionees – most sneezes causing a momentary interruption to the flow of my playing and resulting in the maestro's unhelpful words of encouragement such as 'play properly' – delivered with all the charm of a wellington boot. The moment of inevitability arrived, and I told him I was disappointed that he clearly didn't understand my predicament and that I was leaving. Despite expectations, I did actually get paid by the opera company. The next time I crossed paths with the 'great' man was on stage for an LSO rehearsal. I was not comfortable to see him and assumed that he would either stay out of my way, else come and remonstrate with me, though hopefully not hit me. At the break he strode over to me, shook my hand and said how nice it was to see me. I have a hunch that the greeting would have been less courteous had the situation been different.

The other occasion when a conductor instructed me to 'play properly' remains a mystery. I was in an impossible situation in Maida Vale Studio 2 to play for a conductor's rehearsal with the BBC Singers, in preparation for a Gilbert and Sullivan Prom. Probably by chance, from how things had been set up, Sir Charles Mackerras was sitting on a stool in front of the singers with the piano behind him but to his right, so that he was way behind and to the left of me, meaning that I couldn't see him.

I went to move the piano, and he asked what I was doing. When I explained, he said that it was fine as it was and that we should start. I didn't like to contradict him, so I muddled through until a point where, sight-reading as I was, I missed a change in the speed of his beat. He stopped and said, "Play properly, man." I didn't walk out but calmly replied that the situation was impossible and that I was going to move the piano so that I could see him. He looked daggers at me but said nothing – all completely illogical and with no rational explanation, other than maybe taking some pleasure from exercising control.

Sometimes space becomes a serious problem for orchestras. I remember a number of members of the BBCCO being sent home from the theatre in Barnstable, not long after completing the journey from London, due to a small stage. Back in 2008, the RPO was similarly challenged in Prague for a performance of music from Prokofiev's *Romeo and Juliet*. In the event, the celeste had to be placed on the opposite side of the stage from the piano, causing great amusement to the audience when I had to leave the platform after the first piano entry in *Montagues and Capulets*, run round backstage, then creep back on to play the celeste. At that moment, Charles

Keyboard section set-up in Symphony Hall, Birmingham for a performance of Grainger's *The Warriors*.

Dutoit looked over to his left to acknowledge the celeste entry, heard it from the other side of the stage, swung round to look, and grinned!

One anecdote that was hugely amusing at the time involved Percy Grainger's *The Warriors*. I was rehearsing in Cardiff with the BBC Welsh Orchestra (now BBC NOW) and Richard Hickox for a performance in Birmingham. For some reason, the publishers had not included my part in the set sent to Wales, and they were frantically faxing it to the studio as fast as possible. In practice, that was not really fast enough, and I would busk from a full score whilst waiting for the lethargic electronics to catch up. Meanwhile, two members of BBC staff were frantically juggling the full score and sheets of fax paper that were persistently making a bid for freedom from the music desk. Richard was highly amused, and we joked about this after the rehearsal – also the fact that the piece had everything in it except an organ. When we got to Birmingham the next day, I was delighted to see my chum Adrian Partington sitting at the organ ready to play along – Richard had added an organ part!

Talking about a lack of music reminds me of an occasion with the LSO when I was booked to play the organ for a Bruckner Mass. Now, I was fairly sure that this particular Mass setting didn't have an organ part and I checked with the librarian, Graham Chambers, who confirmed that he didn't have a part. It seemed prudent to turn up anyway, so I left that Sunday morning, stopping to pick up a copy of the *Radio Times* as I knew the concert was being broadcast. My anxiety level rose significantly when I found the listing, showing my name as organist! Arriving at the Barbican, I found the organ but, as anticipated, no music. Eventually I sought out Sir Colin Davis, who was conducting that day, and pointed out that there wasn't an organ part. "No," he said, "but maybe you can find a vocal score and play along where you think it appropriate. I do feel that the organ gives an extra religious quality to the music."

This next memory wasn't strictly an instrument malfunction. I was in Manchester's Bridgewater Hall to record the missing organ part for my Christmas piece *Noel!* for organ and orchestra, the orchestral parts of which had been recorded earlier in the orchestra's rehearsal hall (Hallé St Peter's) – a lovely facility but without an organ. We were set up ready when the engineer discovered a noise coming from one of the lights over the stage. It appeared that it could not be disabled selectively, so there was apparently nothing for it but to turn them all off. This was potentially challenging as the small lamp over the music desk really only lit the music and didn't cover any of the stops or playing aids. I enlisted help from conductor Stephen Bell, who used one hand to push some buttons for me that I couldn't see in the dark, while holding an iPhone in the other hand and using it as a torch!

My last organistic reminiscence is more something of a non-event. Over the years I have been asked to overdub numerous missing organ parts in orchestral recordings and film scores, due to the lack of a suitable instrument during the main recording session. Apart from a few occasions where this was done on location using an electronic instrument, when given the choice I have asked to use the organ in Temple Church, London, for such overdubs. This is a large and very versatile instrument that records really well in the church's wonderful acoustic and sits nicely in the underlying orchestral recording. On one such occasion, I received a phone call from a leading orchestral contractor asking me if I was available to add the big organ part to Hans Zimmer's new score for the 2014 film *Interstellar*. I was asked to suggest a suitable venue, and we also discussed dates. As usual, I requested that we use the organ in Temple Church. Following further phone calls from the contractor, I was somewhat miffed to then receive an indirect message via my diary service, telling me that I wouldn't be needed after all – cowardly and rather disappointing on many levels.

A diary service can be of real help in providing an extra layer of support to musicians and also reassurance to orchestral 'fixers'. In the situation above, it meant that someone didn't have to talk to me and explain why they had reneged on their invitation. The two giants in this specialist field of musicians' support are Morgensterns and MAS (the Musician's Answering Service). The first diary service I used no longer works with musicians and was something of a disaster, being run by staff who unfortunately had little or no understanding of the profession. Things frequently went wrong and a favourite moment was getting a call to say that an engagement had been accepted for me to play "One, eight, one, two" – they apparently hadn't heard of the *1812 Overture*!

I mentioned having worked on many concerts and recordings with John Scott, director of music at St Paul's Cathedral and later, St Thomas Church, Fifth Avenue, New York. There was a period in the early noughties when the BBCCO presented several concerts featuring the choir of St Paul's Cathedral, singing Fauré's Requiem, followed by Saint-Saëns' *Organ Symphony* in the second half; the usual format being that John would play the organ for the Fauré and Saint-Saëns. On one occasion, in St Paul's Cathedral itself, co-pianist Alistair Young and I wandered back down the nave of the cathedral when we had finished rehearsing our duet section, in order to enjoy the sonic experience of the rest of the finale. Those who know this instrument will be able to imagine our reaction when we reached the slow *'maestoso'* section and out came all the organ's west-end fanfare trumpets – total obliteration of anything else in the building! We wandered down to see John at the break, and he asked how it was sounding. I think our stunned expressions must have still been in place. "Ah … " he said, with a slight grin – he was having a bit of fun, of course, and knew perfectly well what he was doing!

This programme also featured in something of a musical pantomime in the Fairfield Halls, Croydon. On this occasion, Vernon (Tod) Handley was due to conduct the programme. Unfortunately, he cancelled at the eleventh hour, and I arrived in Croydon to be greeted by Ian Maclay, the general manager at the time, and the principal horn, Stephen Bell, who by then had done a considerable amount of conducting. Ian's plan was that I would play the organ for the Fauré and that John would conduct. I would then move back to the piano for the *Organ Symphony*, John would move to the organ, and Steve, who had only ever played this piece, would move from his horn seat to the rostrum to conduct. This was the ultimate musical chairs, and a story that always arose when John and I met up – it was a fun concert, if somewhat 'edge of the seat'! We always enjoyed working with Tod, who was a mine of musical knowledge and blessed with a terrific sense of humour. It was fascinating to hear him recount, in preparation for a performance of Elgar's *Enigma Variations*, that in the first published edition of the work, *Nimrod* was actually marked faster, around *andante*. It was only when the composer realised the commercial possibilities of the now traditional slower tempo, that the printed tempo marking was revised to *adagio*.

The last occasion that I met up with John Scott was in 2010 for a drink at the Southgate Bar in New York, close to the Choir School. Apart from our traditional reminiscence about the 'Saint-Saëns Saga', John also recounted, with a mixture of disbelief and frustration, how, not long previously, he had turned up at the RAH for a night-time rehearsal in preparation for one of the periodic organ recitals to find that another recitalist had arranged to take over his rehearsal slot. John was clearly less than happy about the situation and, maybe in an attempt to appease him, his adversary offered him a complimentary ticket to his recital – John was not amused!

I've spent much of my life combining my love of music with my interest in electronics. In fact, I've always struggled somewhat with having too many interests, and I know this was sometimes a problem whilst at college when trying to find time to do my four hours' daily practice! More recently, the technical has met the musical by way of computers and electronic keyboards, and I have spent much time creating specific sound samples (short recordings that you can play back by using a keyboard) for concerts and recordings. These have included the nightingale bird-call for Respighi's *Pines of Rome* and the bells for Berlioz's *Symphonie Fantastique*, the latter for an RPO recording as well as live performances in the RFH with the LPO and Zubin Mehta. This involved placing several large speaker cabinets high up in the hall in areas you're not usually allowed to access – very exciting, of course. More recently, another venture has involved providing specialist organ sounds, and these have been incorporated to great effect in a number of film scores as well as orchestral recordings and concerts.

Early setup for the 'cannons' • *Othello* • LSO/Barbican (2009)

Although none of these electronic activities has failed or caused any fatalities, there was a very exciting time some years ago with the BBCCO (2011). The orchestra knew that I had previously created some samples of cannon fire to use at the Barbican for performances of *Othello* (2009) with the LSO and Sir Colin Davis, and I was invited to join them for a performance of Beethoven's *Wellington's Victory (Battle Symphony)*, just behind the Wellington Arch at Hyde Park Corner. This was to be conducted by Brian Wright. We were set up in good time, ready to set a level in the public address system for the audience. When indicated, I fired off a few volleys by way of a test. Unfortunately, the front of house engineer had left my level set extremely high, and the effect, to say the least, was dramatic. Flocks of birds launched themselves from the trees in Buckingham Palace Garden, beyond Birdcage Walk, and passers-by stopped in their tracks, if they hadn't actually taken cover. I have no idea what the unsuspecting members of the royal household might have thought about these musical explosions!

Have I mentioned the near-death experiences? Maybe I exaggerate just a little, but on two separate occasions I thought my time might be up. Both during RPO tours, although that is pure coincidence. The first occurred while onboard an internal flight in Spain. In fact, I shouldn't have been on the tour at all, as I was booked on the basis of there being two keyboard players in Prokofiev's *Romeo and Juliet*. Actually, the movements being performed only needed one player, but I kept up the pretence so as not to cause embarrassment. On one of the legs of the trip, we were on our approach to A Coruña, in terrible weather. We suddenly came through the cloud base to see the runway approaching us at an alarming speed, and the plane immediately pulled up. After a brief moment, the captain spoke to us very excitedly in Spanish – this was a charter flight, and we were all English. A stewardess translated, "The captain has just explained that he tried to land at A Coruña without success and is going to try again." At this point, the managing director of the orchestra headed straight down the plane to the flight deck saying, "Oh no he's not!" We were diverted to Santiago de Compostela and a coach arranged for the onward journey.

The other occasion was a 'hit and run' to La Scala, Milan – we had left London that morning for a rehearsal and concert, then headed straight back to the airport. Unwisely, the charter company had decided to slip in an extra booking during the day – that proved to be a bad and costly decision. By the time they attempted to fly back into Milan, the weather was too bad to land, and we spent most of that night on benches at the airport, eventually taking off at around 7:00am. Unfortunately, there was also very bad weather when we got close to Stansted. We had one aborted landing and went round again – all extremely worrying. All the more so, as looking at the seasoned cabin crew in their seats, we could see the whites of their knuckles as they gripped the armrests!

Not all such experiences need to involve a runway. In late 2013, I was travelling from Euston to Glasgow with my wife and an orchestra in

Coach replacement service failure, Preston to Carlisle (late 2013)

the safety and comfort of a train. As we headed north, the weather became more and more treacherous, and we eventually stopped at (I think) Preston, where we had to wait for a bus replacement service to take us onwards. Eventually we boarded a coach, and Jo and I were sitting in the front seats. The weather increasingly deteriorated – violent gusts of wind and torrential rain, and we were being blown around quite forcefully.

Trying to look cool ...

This wasn't, perhaps, the most appropriate time for the driver to be consulting his schedule, from the middle lane of the M6, at 60mph – quite terrifying.

The weather can have a direct effect on our ability not only to get to work, but also to carry out our duties. Extremes of temperature can occur from time to time. Very high temperatures can cause problems, particularly with stringed instruments, as the glue can soften. On one RPO trip to Annecy with the music director the heat in the church was intense and any sense of decorum went out of the window – the formality of clothes being swiftly dispensed with. Rain can also cause problems for outdoor concerts when entering the performing area. On one occasion I was with the BBC in Pembroke Castle, and the cloud base was so low that the electronics in my keyboard set-up were fizzing merrily! Many rehearsals have been abandoned due to extremes of weather. Some outdoor concerts have actually had to be cancelled, although audiences seem content to sit and get soaked. On another occasion, I was performing alongside my wife, and the December temperature plummeted so low that many of us were resorting to the comfort of outdoor clothing! You can usually rely on a cathedral to add a little chill to proceedings, but this was a regular performance venue. We suspect the added cost of heating had not been factored in by the promoter. They did, however, provide a terrific meal to try and make amends!

I'm indebted to my friend and ex-Radio 3 producer Fiona Shelmerdine for reminding me of a rather fun failure that occurred during a Prom in 1999 – *100 Years of Film Music*. The programme included Malcolm Arnold's famous march from the film *The Bridge on the River Kwai*, for which I was joined for the piano-duet part by Leslie Pearson. Of more significance is the fact that the tune is initially played by a harmonica. For reasons unknown, the player engaged was not available until the rehearsal break, and when the moment came to rehearse the march, he seemed unfamiliar with the tune and was reluctant to play it. It was therefore decided that the Prommers would be invited to whistle it, which, of course, they did with great enthusiasm and aplomb!

I'll finish this chapter with a little memory from Shanghai. I was leaving the hotel for the second half of a rehearsal and planning to get a taxi. In the foyer I met Brian Thompson, then principal trumpet, who was making the same journey but by underground and, against my better instincts, I decided to join him. We ended up in the main square, and Brian pointed confidently at a building. Unfortunately, when we went in, all we found were local people watching an old black-and-white film. Much pidgin English and shrugging of shoulders ensued and several more similar buildings were visited, all called the People's Theatre. We called Graham Midgley, the RPO's tours manager extraordinaire, who told us to look for a tall white building. This vast square was lined by exceedingly tall trees, and nothing else could be seen. The issue for me was the repertoire – Korngold's Violin Concerto with a hugely prominent celeste part. We eventually found the theatre, totally breathless, and having missed the whole rehearsal. I sought out Charles Dutoit to apologise – he looked stern, then he smiled and said, "Did you not have your satnav?"

Lastly, a failure for good manners. There's a saying that you occasionally hear in orchestral circles – "Better sharp than out of tune." A celebrity soloist, famous for playing sharp, came on stage to rehearse with the LSO. The principal oboist gave him an 'A' to tune, and he said, "What do you call that?" He lost any goodwill he might have had at the start, which was probably not much, following previous appearances.

14 – The Royal Philharmonic Orchestra

My first engagement with the Royal Philharmonic Orchestra came in the mid-eighties with a concert in Gloucester Cathedral, as part of the Three Choirs Festival. This was to play piano two in Stravinsky's *Symphony of Psalms,* piano one being played by the indefatigable Michael Round. Michael has become a good friend, and I have always admired not just his remarkable technique and quick wit, but also his prodigious knowledge of music. At that time I was living in Ilford, and it had been arranged that I would pick up the cor anglais player, Victoria Walpole, from her home in north London. This was our first meeting and, if you haven't skipped over any earlier chapters, you'll know that we later became good friends.

I had met the principal keyboard player for the RPO, Vivian Troon, on previous occasions, but at that time he was on holiday. All went well, and before long I was invited back to the orchestra for further concerts, usually working alongside Viv or Michael, although sometimes alone when they were not available – this was most frequently during August, when Viv's family went to their beloved Great Bernera on Lewis in the Outer Hebrides. Viv became a dear friend in the years to come, when we spent a great deal of time socialising, playing and touring together.

One exciting collaboration was in 1994 for the solo piano parts in the RPO's recording of *The Carnival of the Animals.* This was made for the Tring label at the CTS Studios. This recording has subsequently been licensed to many other labels and still appears to be going strong. Tring was the brainchild of violinist Alan Peters, who was acting as producer. However, when we were about to start the Saint-Saëns he turned to the engineer, Dick Lewzey and said, "You can do this one."

Now, Dick is one of the most experienced and successful engineers you could wish to meet and quite capable of keeping an ear on the music, having recorded a considerable number of mainstream albums and films over the years. However, on this occasion he rather had his hands full, so Viv and I co-produced, as by now Alan had inexplicably left the situation.

Sometimes I joined an RPO trip in the middle, and when I reached the hotel, Viv would be sitting at a table in the hotel bar with two glasses of Scotch, having carefully researched my schedule and anticipated my arrival time. The Troons lived in Kenton in Middlesex, where I was a not infrequent visitor over the years, getting to know his wife, the clarinettist Angela Fussell, and their two children, Fiona and Malcolm. Viv retired from the orchestra in the late nineties, and I was very proud to carry forward the mantle of his position (unofficially) for some twenty years.

Over the years, I was privileged to make numerous solo recordings with the RPO, including de Falla's *Nights in the Gardens of Spain*, Hubert Bath's *Cornish Rhapsody*, Miklós Rózsa's *Spellbound Concerto* and, of course, Richard Addinsell's *Warsaw Concerto*. This work actually owes a huge amount to its unsung orchestrator, Roy Douglas, who rarely gets a mention. I recorded this, together with *Spellbound Concerto,* at Watford Colosseum in September 2005 with the eminent conductor, José Serebrier. Mr Serebrier appears to have a serious dislike of recording aids such as red lights and take numbering, the consequence of that being something of a headache for the production crew. The engineer and producer team of Tony Faulkner and Anna Barry did us proud, and at the time of writing, our recording of *Warsaw Concerto* is still a Classic FM favourite. For many years, and for reasons that are still not known, this was routinely broadcast without any credit to the pianist. Eventually this was put right and one Christmas I received all the back royalties. Not remotely a huge amount, as some seem to believe, but I like to say that on that occasion, all my Christmases did come at once! I have performed the piece with many orchestras over the years, but frequently with the RPO and conductor, Barry Wordsworth, usually in combination with *Cornish Rhapsody.*

The other big solo on this recording, *Spellbound Concerto,* is conceived on a grand scale, involving a solo piano with a large orchestra including a celeste (played on the RPO recording by my wife, Jo), as well as the novelty of a theremin (played by Celia Sheen) – a curious electronic instrument making a very distinctive sound that can be heard on the signature tune for *Midsomer Murders.* This RPO recording also includes the suite from *Casablanca* with the famous 'As time goes by'. After many years of rather naughtily tinkling this tune whilst waiting for a late-arriving conductor, I was at last able to play it on stage legitimately.

It was a pleasure to perform *Warsaw Concerto* with the orchestra and José Serebrier at the Royal Albert Hall in November 2015. Contrary to what might be imagined, I have always found it to be a very warm and comfortable experience sitting at the front of this particular platform, all the more so when surrounded by friends as well as my old pal Tommy Pearson, who was compèring this concert and whom I've known from when he worked for BBC Radio 3. Always good company and a fount of knowledge, especially in all matters relating to films and their composers.

In 2001, the Royal Albert Hall mounted a celebratory performance of Mahler's Eighth Symphony (that *Symphony of a Thousand* again and No. 10 for me). This was sponsored by J.P. Morgan, whose head office, by coincidence, is now located in my old school building on Victoria Embankment. This performance was conducted by Owain Arwel Hughes, who had a long-standing relationship with the orchestra and was principal associate conductor for several years. He has conducted the orchestra widely in this country and also in Wales for the Welsh Proms in Cardiff, which he founded in 1986. His *The Much Loved Music Show* ran on BBC TV between 1978 and 1982 and was responsible for drawing many people into the world of classical music. The orchestra made a recording of Holst's *The Planets* with him in Watford Colosseum (2004), and I always had a soft spot for this CD. Also memorable on this recording is the ethereal and beautifully pitched singing of the ladies from John Rutter's Cambridge Singers. Owain always brings enthusiasm and passion to his music-making, and he is also a great pragmatist. This particular performance of Mahler's *Symphony of a Thousand* was to be mounted with minimal rehearsal, and Owain's approach was to make it safe for performance and sort as many issues as practical. We actually finished the final rehearsal quite early and approached the performance with a level of confidence that was quite reassuring. This has not always been the case with this piece when in other hands ...

I worked extensively with both of the recent music directors of the RPO – Daniele Gatti and Charles Dutoit. Sadly, these gentlemen have both experienced accusations of misconduct against women resulting, most recently, in Dutoit's departure from the RPO in 2018. I toured a good deal with Gatti and the RPO in the late nineties, frequently performing either

Prokofiev's ballet suites from *Romeo and Juliet* or Respighi's *Fountains of Rome*. His concerts could be electrifying, though he was quite unreasonable at times, and drove the stage crew mad with unrealistic demands for orchestral layouts that were not practical. Sadly, this led to the dismissal of one of our most popular and experienced stage managers when he was driven to the end of his tether; telling the maestro, unambiguously, and very publicly, what he thought of his ideas – a great loss.

On at least two occasions on tour, when the tour management company had provided a hire celeste (in particular, I remember, for *Fountains of Rome* and Shostakovich's Fifth Symphony), the instrument was found wanting – they can be quite unreliable. Gatti would rarely take on board the reality of the situation, but instead he would attack me verbally, as though it was somehow my fault and I should be able to fix it! I remember that on one occasion for the celeste solo at the end of the first movement of Shostakovich's Fifth Symphony, and in order to preserve both the musical flow and the ceasefire, my good friend and principal percussionist Stephen Quigley quietly covered the celeste notes on his glockenspiel, as not all the notes on the celeste were working.

Ordinarily, playing someone else's part is not something we would or should do. However, it's become increasingly common for keyboard players to be asked to cover a guitar or harp part if an orchestra does not want to pay for a player for just one or two pieces. The principle is that you should programme music that is playable by the players engaged for the concert. Covering missing players simply deprives others of their livelihood and sets a very bad precedent. The only time I would consider doing this is if there is a genuine emergency.

My first concert with Charles Dutoit was before he took up his role as music director of the RPO, and this was for a performance of the same Shostakovich symphony on the stage of La Scala, Milan. His approach was quite different from Gatti's; much less the showman, and also a terrific orchestral trainer. He always kept his beat moving, unlike Gatti, who would frequently stop beating at moments of quiet emotional passion, which could be quite challenging – especially when performing on tour without any real rehearsal and in an unknown performance space.

The magical Palau de la Música Catalana in Barcelona, Spain (2014)

Dutoit's first concerts as music director came in the autumn of 2008, when a sizeable RPO embarked on a European tour. The repertoire included Prokofiev's *Romeo and Juliet* and the original version of Stravinsky's *Petrushka* – this includes large wind and percussion forces as well as three harps and three keyboard players. For this, my wife joined Alistair Young for the celeste duet, and I played the solo piano part. Charles was very gracious to me, and it proved to be a very rewarding experience, albeit a tiring one, with exceptionally early starts every day.

On some occasions the orchestra would be joined by the pianist, Martha Argerich, one of Charles Dutoit's ex-wives. I spent part of a Prom in the RAH Gallery, listening to her performance of Ravel's G major Concerto – pure magic. During Dutoit's time as music director we gave many performances of *Mother Goose*, *Valse Nobles et Sentimentales* and *Daphnis et Chloé*; both the second suite and the complete ballet, which I remember performing with him in the stunning Palau de la Música Catalana in Barcelona. This is a relatively small space and the large orchestra extended out towards the audience. Charles would periodically get a bee in his bonnet about a particular instrument, and when he was on a roll, I think most of us wondered whether it would be our turn next. On this occasion, he was nagging away at the harp section; however, the lovely Hugh Webb wasn't having any of it and fielded the attack most impressively.

Dutoit could be exceedingly demanding, especially with regard to dynamics and tone colour. Orchestras can be reluctant to voluntarily play a real pianissimo, frequently for good reasons of performance safety, but he could be insistent and nag away until he achieved it. When touring *Mother Goose* you could rely on him to spend a significant period, in limited rehearsal time, on just the opening bars of the final movement, *Le jardin féerique*, with its hushed and delicate string textures. This work also has lovely celeste writing, but you need a good instrument. I remember we were in Rimini for a performance in a tent which included this beautiful work. The local celeste was terrible, but in strict contrast to the frequently unreasonable verbal attacks of Daniele Gatti, Charles said nothing in rehearsal. During the orchestral break, I had gone down to the dressing room, and when walking back upstairs I saw Charles coming the other way. He said hello and asked after my health in his usual charming way, and then went to walk past. As he passed me, he turned and said, "About the celeste ..." He smiled and walked on. He knew there was nothing to be done and that I probably felt badly about it.

Charles Dutoit always seemed to me to be very aware of stage courtesies. I left the platform after a remarkable performance of Respighi's *Roman Trilogy* in the 2014 Proms, in which I had also operated

Montreux tour (2016)

the playback machine for the famous 'nightingale' solo (for which I received a glowing press review!). Part two of the trilogy, *Pines of Rome,* has some exquisite and atmospheric piano solos. Unusually, Charles had omitted to acknowledge me at the end of the performance, and although I was not at all concerned by this, he spoke to me as I came offstage and apologised –

Birthday lunch for Jo (l-r) Matthew, Jo, Suzy Willison-Kawalec, Gerald Kirby, Alistair Young, Stephen Quigley and Richard 'Dickie' Horne (2012)

I was quite touched. However, and somewhat surprisingly, there was a major faux pas from the maestro after a performance of Ravel's *Boléro* in Montreux. This piece is driven by an insistent and not unchallenging side-drum figure played from start to finish; one that always demands an acknowledgement for the percussionist at the end. For some reason, Charles never acknowledged Stephen Quigley's solo, and I don't think he ever realised his oversight.

Despite the challenges, I will always be grateful for having had the opportunity to rehearse and perform the music of Ravel with this perceptive musician.

Nestling on the picturesque banks of Lake Geneva, the annual visit to the summer festival in Montreux was a highlight for the RPO and one that continued for quite a few years – beautiful scenery, excellent eating opportunities, fine hotels and lovely music-making. On one occasion Alistair Young flew out to play the organ part for Bartók's *Duke Bluebeard's Castle.* There's a section in this work, close to the end, where a solo horn is accompanied by just a delicate and very pure organ tone. Unfortunately, this was one of those moments with which, as for *Mother Goose,* Dutoit had something of an intimate 'affection'. The organ supplied was totally inadequate for the job – a very small electronic instrument that had been provided and set up by a firm which clearly had no concept of what was required – somewhat reminiscent of my experience with the LSO in Perugia for Brahms' Requiem. Unfortunately, there were only two or three quiet stops on the organ, and none of them made remotely the sort of sound required for this special moment. Quite unreasonably, Dutoit made a big issue about this, both in rehearsal and during the break, and somewhat reminiscent of his predecessor, seemed surprisingly unable to grasp that there was absolutely nothing that Alistair could do to remedy the situation. Some conductors have little or no understanding of the nature of an organ – what's possible and what isn't. Some like to give the impression that they know a good deal about the instrument but by doing so, only prove that they know very little or nothing! An organ doesn't have an infinite tonal palette. This made for a very uncomfortable atmosphere for all concerned, and I know Alistair felt very badly about this, although he was blameless.

When the same piece arose in the Proms a few years later, and I was due to be playing the organ (Jo was playing the celeste part), I began to get a sense of foreboding. At the start of the RAH rehearsal, it became clear that it was my turn for a little of the special Dutoit attention! We had all assembled on stage, but before starting, Charles asked whether he could hear the organ alone for that passage. I played him what I had prepared, but he wasn't happy – I tried another sound only to be greeted by another impatient shake of the head. He requested several more options with an increasing rapidity that was equal and opposite to my ability to change the stops before his next downbeat, resulting in obvious frustration on his part when I couldn't meet his demand in time – a demand that was pretty well equal to my own increasing sense of discomfort and anxiety.

One of the problems with the situation in the RAH is that of verbal communication. With Charles at a fair distance from the organ loft, it was difficult to tactfully explain that I needed a brief moment between each trial in order to push in one stop and draw another. Somehow we kept going without relations breaking down and worked our way, albeit falteringly, through the roughly dozen or so possibilities for this sound. However, the moment of realisation came – we were heading, inexorably, towards the point when I would run out of options. The moment came, and not for the first time in such a situation, I had no choice but to select the stop with which I had started the process, one that was based on my own instinct and knowledge of the organ – he beamed and said this one was good. Hey ho, 'twas ever thus!

I sympathise with conductors who don't understand the nature of an organ and how it works. They might, quite reasonably, assume that stops available on one instrument will sound the same on another, leading to the sort of situation just described. Unfortunately, this is simply not the case, as each organ is designed differently, with its tonal palette crafted for a particular acoustic or style of performance. I can understand that when working in an unfamiliar hall, or with an unknown organ, a conductor might reasonably like to have an idea of what sounds are available. Like many of my colleagues, I have occasionally been asked to give up my break to show the conductor what options exist for a particularly prominent or characterful part – something I've always been happy to do. However, the likelihood is that when the rest of the orchestra joins the organ, it will probably be too quiet and may also sound different. What is particularly irksome, as has happened, is to be told, across the orchestra, that you must do what was agreed, rather giving the impression to colleagues that you're being unprofessional and something of a 'naughty boy'!

In the 2018 Proms, I was playing Henry Wood's orchestration of *The Great Gate of Kiev*, the finale of *Pictures at an Exhibition*. This has a very quiet section for solo organ. In the score, Sir Henry indicated the very stop that he wanted to hear from the RAH organ (the Great Diapason V), an organ he knew well. I was able to forestall any debate about this by advising the conductor of this fact before the rehearsal in the hall!

There were some extraordinary tours in the 'noughties'. These included trips to pastures new, such as being the first major orchestra to visit Kazakhstan (May 2002) and a unique opportunity, at the post-concert reception, to unwittingly eat things about which you would rather not know. There was also a first trip to Azerbaijan (July 2010) and Armenia (September 2010). We had a particularly fun trip to Turkey to play in the Great Theatre at Ephesus (June 2007). Here we stayed in the all-inclusive Hotel de Luxe near Aydin – the all-inclusive aspect being warmly greeted by many members of the orchestra until they discovered, rather too late, that this aspect of the bar had ceased at midnight! The conductor was Gennady Rozhdestvensky – a musical genius and something of a clown. I remember a performance of Stravinsky's *The Firebird* ballet with the LSO in the Barbican when, for the opening bars in twelve, he circled his beat around his head as though proscribing the circumference of a horizontal clock. In *Petrushka*, one bar ahead of the poignant solo contrabassoon note, he would turn to face the audience; at the point of the explosive F sharp entry, he would make a jabbing gesture at the instrument over his shoulder, resulting in much hilarity from the audience. 'Noddy', as he was affectionately known, was not renowned for his love of rehearsal and was frequently in trouble for curtailing them, especially when dealing with less well-known repertoire. On at least one occasion, he tried to cancel a whole day of rehearsals and had to be persuaded to change his mind due to the not-so-familiar repertoire in the programme.

To deviate for a moment, I remember a very funny moment with Noddy and the LSO in April 1994, prior to a recording session in Blackheath Halls. We were recording the *Missa Sabrinensis* by the greatly respected English composer Herbert Howells (I have heard this piece very unkindly nicknamed *The Gloucester Bore*). The maestro was holding court with some members of the London Symphony Chorus who had asked him what he thought of the music. The maestro calmly turned his score to page one and considered it ... he turned a couple of pages, looked thoughtful again, pointed and said, "Zees good bar." He turned a few more pages, stopped to point and again said, "Zees also good bar." He carried on in this vein a few more times until he reached the final page and pointing to the final bar, he said, "Zees best bar!"

Very unkind, of course, but it brought a degree of mirth from his audience. I think that this particular style of writing was just not for him. The recordings were originally to have been conducted by Richard Hickox, but for certain practical reasons, the plan was changed. I think Richard's take on the music would have been somewhat different.

Meanwhile, in Turkey, we actually rehearsed in the hotel, due to the daytime heat at the venue, and this might count as the quickest walk to work (in close competition with that from the Brucknerhaus in Linz

The Grand Theatre, Ephesus, Turkey (June 2007)

to the adjacent hotel). A highlight of the day was having most of the morning and the whole afternoon in the hotel – the hotel overlooked the Mediterranean, and there were abundant and paid-for refreshments on tap and all sorts of watersports. Bikinis came out, and the hotel pools were challenged in no small measure. With so many attractions on offer, we might have been forgiven for thinking that we were on holiday. I was wandering around with my chum Gerald Kirby from the percussion section and, perhaps rashly, we decided to try parascending. I have no idea how high we went, but it was the most fantastic experience. Certainly something I'd not previously tried, even in our wilder adventures at Glasbury outdoor pursuits centre.

Other tours included Macau, Taiwan, Japan, Dubai and several to China with Charles Dutoit, frequently joined by the quite extraordinary talent of the young pianist Yuja Wang. At the time of writing, it's quite

significant to remember the disturbing open meat markets in places like Shanghai and Beijing. April 2012 included a very brief trip to Beijing with the Royal Philharmonic Concert Orchestra, held in the National (Olympic) Stadium. In true pioneering spirit,

Parascending with Gerald Kirby • Aydin, Turkey (June 2007)

A few too many notes reluctant to rise to the occasion • Beijing (2012)

following an eleven-hour overnight flight and braving the yellow pollution over the city, the orchestra went almost straight into a rehearsal. The conductor was Michael Seal – for many years a violinist in the CBSO but now forging a highly successful and well-deserved career as a conductor. The next morning we rehearsed in the venue, but due to the strength of the sun, and the inability of an array of staff with umbrellas to prevent it shining on the instruments at the front of the stage, the rehearsal had to be abandoned as the glue in the instruments was starting to soften. We reassembled for a hastily arranged pre-concert rehearsal, but no one had told the security staff, so much of that time was also lost, as they wouldn't let us in! The conditions had apparently also affected the celeste, which had a number of notes suffering from heatstroke and failing to sit up properly.

For reasons I never established, I had been asked to play Chopin's posthumous Prelude in C sharp minor in that concert. Just before I went on to play it, I received the news that our organist colleague, John Birch, had passed away, following a stroke some days earlier. That performance became hugely poignant.

John's funeral (15th May 2012) was a truly remarkable and spiritual occasion. At his request, a High Mass of Requiem was sung for him at All Saints Church, Margaret Street in London, where he had been organist in the mid-fifties. I can't imagine there were many cathedral organists on duty that evening – all the great and good of the church and organ world were in attendance to honour this esteemed man and pillar of our profession. The choir sang Duruflé's setting of the Requiem Mass (as explicitly requested by John) most movingly under the sensitive direction of Paul Brough, with Charles Andrews playing the demanding organ accompaniment. At the conclusion, John's former pupil Stephen Disley, a regular visitor to the RPO and sub-organist at Southwark Cathedral, played the famous and extremely challenging organ solo from Janáček's *Glagolitic Mass*. A tour de force at the best of times, but all the more so with the assembled company – a wonderful tribute to John's memory.

The sermon was preached by the Dean of Chichester, the Very Reverend Nicholas Frayling, and I can't pass up the opportunity to share a paragraph from that sermon which, I believe, would have tickled John immensely, as it did the congregation. His reference dates from the time when John was organist and master of the choristers at Chichester Cathedral:

> *"The more daring of the choristers referred to John as 'God', and one,*
> *returning after a few years, met Dean (Walter) Hussey and said,*
> *'Excuse me, Mr Dean, do you know where I might find God?'*
> *'Young man,' replied Hussey, 'God is everywhere:*
> *Mr Birch is everywhere except Chichester.'"*

There are many stories relating to John Birch. One personal anecdote is from a trip that he and I made for a performance of Saint-Saëns' *Organ Symphony* in Bucharest (September 2009), for which I was joined, once again, by Alistair Young for the piano-duet section of the finale. The good

folk in Romania had provided John with a relatively modest electronic organ that only had internal loudspeakers – nothing like enough power to fight off the RPO. After much cajoling, the hall staff found a couple of small keyboard monitors that they put up on stands and fed from a microphone in front of the organ's speakers! This was still woefully inadequate compared with the battery of speakers to

The irrepressible John Birch • Bucharest (September 2009)

be expected, and, of course, there was hardly any bass. John found the whole situation hilarious – almost a case of 'music minus one' and on this occasion, the minus one should have been the most significant part.

For a great many years, John was an honorary member of, and organist to, the RPO. He was formally organist at Chichester Cathedral and, later, Temple Church. John was a great character and raconteur – keeping us entertained for hours. He was curator of the organ in the Royal Albert Hall and, amongst other occasions, he had played for the series of *Classical Spectacular* concerts since their inception and which are promoted twice a year by Raymond Gubbay Ltd. When John passed away I was privileged to inherit this engagement, which I very much enjoy. Not a traditional concert, with its lighting, smoke generators, lasers and reinforced sound; more a sensual experience, but one that gives considerable pleasure to more than five thousand people for each of the six or seven performances that are given twice yearly in March and November.

I'm very lucky to spend so much time playing the Royal Albert Hall's famous and quite wonderful organ, especially when you consider who has also sat on the organ bench – the likes of Anton Bruckner, Charles-Marie Widor and Camille Saint-Saëns. Obviously the power is exciting, but it's actually the breadth of the quieter and deeper sounds that are a real delight, enabling authenticity to a romantic orchestral score that is not possible in many other concert halls – certainly not in London. Strangely, the only time I ever felt intimidated whilst playing this organ was for a BBC television recording of the fortieth anniversary of *Songs of Praise*. On that occasion, the boys of St Paul's Cathedral were appearing for a couple of solo features, the second of which segued into the hymn 'Guide Me, O Thou Great Redeemer'. Their director, John Scott, organist at St Paul's and also for this TV recording, was nervous about getting back to the organ in time following one of these solos and asked whether I would play this hymn arrangement for him. When the moment came, I was poised ready to play, but became aware of John looking over my right shoulder. I offered to move, but he gestured to go ahead. I should not have felt nervous, all the more so as I had worked with him on many previous occasions and we were friends, but somehow, this felt like his territory!

One little tradition in *Classical Spectacular* is the 'segue' from *Rule Britannia!* (organ) to *Nessun Dorma* (affectionately nicknamed *Des 'n Norma*). The latter has a small but colourful part for the celeste, and on these particular occasions, the instrument is situated behind the violins, almost offstage in the bull run. Whilst there has always been an indicated spoken link at that point, I've never known it happen, and over the years it has become a badge of honour to run as fast as possible from the organ, down two flights of stairs, to reach the celeste in time for the first entry. Occasionally an overzealous member of the security staff can try to slow things down, by demanding to see a pass at the top of the stairs, but the entry has not been missed, even when there's been a gaggle of soloists lurking behind the stage entrance, seemingly unable to see the urgency of the situation. There's always a knowing beam from the conductor (currently the lovely John Rigby) when he hears that first chord!

Early in 2012, my good friend and former organ pupil Mauro Sheehan asked whether I would be able to play for his wedding to Vanessa on the 8th of August. I've always felt it a privilege to play for friends' special occasions, be they happy or sad. However, on this occasion I was already committed to a second trip with the orchestra to Azerbaijan, and from there to travel on to Shanghai for concerts with the music director. As sometimes happens, life jumped in, and I was told that for

The wonderful view from the organ loft in the Royal Albert Hall.

Approach to Heathrow during the Olympics (2012)

programming reasons I was no longer required in China. That was disappointing, but it did mean that Jo and I had a very special day in Hornchurch, attending the wedding of this lovely couple. I've found many times over the years that life can jump in and provide a silver lining for an initial disappointment – some might call it karma.

This trip to Azerbaijan ended for me in quite a nerve-racking way – a three-hour taxi ride at high speed in the company of three strangers, by way of the perilous coastal road from Gabala to the airport at Baku. I'd been warned about this journey by the orchestra's librarian, Patrick Williams, who also cautioned me not to let anyone at the airport help me with my luggage, as I may not see it again! A small bonus was flying into Heathrow across the foot of the Docklands peninsula with a most spectacular view of the Olympic Park.

The 2013 tour to China started just a couple of days after our house move from Ilford to Thundersley, and I remember a considerable sense of guilt in fleeing the country for the best part of three weeks with the house piled high with boxes. I had spent all my life living in Ilford, barely a mile from the bottom of the M11. When Jo and I married in 2007, we always planned to move and continue life in a home that we had bought together. As much as I tried, after twenty-three years living in my last house opposite Valentines Park, it was hard to give up old habits of making small changes without consultation! The final impetus came from our son Matthew's impending move from nursery to primary school. Initially, we had been looking around the general areas of

Brentwood and Billericay, but were unable to find anywhere that suited us. We really wanted somewhere with a good-sized room to be a music room that would house all the paraphernalia of two busy, itinerant musicians. We therefore looked further out and eventually happened upon our new home in Thundersley – the 'Far East', as I like to call it – exchanging contracts with just two days to go until the cut-off date for the schools' selection process. We are lucky to now have a separate room as a studio, which also houses our combined music libraries and other instruments. When we moved in, this area was being used as a games room and had a dilapidated bar in the corner. The builders were horrified at the prospect of taking this out and offered to create a new bar at the far end. I'm no artist, but I did spend much of a quiet morning's rehearsal sitting at the piano and, when not needed, making a sketch for a new bar – much to the amusement of my colleagues!

One final anecdote – we were in the RAH for an opera gala with a certain Italian conductor. Mid-rehearsal, I had the organ on with the console lights blazing, ready to play the Intermezzo from Mascagni's *Cavalleria Rusticana*. Now, the physical presence of the organ in the RAH is not subtle, but this maestro looked up from his score to say, with his best Italian accent, "Do wee 'av an organ?"

Montreux tour (2016)

15 – This 'n That

I've not made mention of the other main symphony orchestra in London – the Philharmonia. As is the way of things in this profession, I've not had the pleasure of working much with this respected orchestra. In 1989, I was recommended by the orchestra's long-standing principal keyboard player Leslie Pearson to play the organ for two performances of Mozart's Requiem (RFH and St David's Hall, Cardiff), conducted by the eminent Carlo Maria Giulini.

I think it's only natural to feel a slight sense of apprehension on the first occasion that you cross paths with such a legend of the music world, even if common sense says that this is completely illogical. It was therefore a source of some concern when, at the prior rehearsal in Henry Wood Hall, Borough (a favourite venue for many rehearsals and recordings), the great man walked in and headed straight to the organ. Did he have a sixth sense that I was about to do something wrong? He shook my hand and said, "Good evening. Please not to use the basses." By this he was simply asking me not to use the pedals on the organ to double the orchestral bass line, which I wasn't about to do, but of which he clearly had prior experience. With that, he walked off and subsequently directed two quite magical performances to capacity audiences.

A completely different opportunity arose for me in the early seventies, when I received an invitation to go to Deal and perform a concerto with the Royal Marines. Strange, I thought, my mind initially running riot at the thought of performing Tchaikovsky's Piano Concerto No. 1 with a military band. What I didn't appreciate was that the Royal Marines School of Music (which, in 1989, was to be a tragic victim of the IRA's campaign on the mainland) also had a very fine symphony orchestra, conducted by the Royal Marines principal director of music Lt Col Paul Neville. Paul was a very good friend to me, and I became a regular visitor to Deal for concerto engagements, both on piano and organ. For a few years, I also joined the Massed Bands of Her Majesty's Royal Marines at the Royal Albert Hall, playing the organ for the annual Mountbatten Festival of Music. Musically, this was quite curious as some repertoire, with which I was very familiar, had been transposed into flat keys to suit the rest of the performers. I was privileged to meet Lord Louis Mountbatten on two occasions, and on the second occasion he greeted me in the interval reception with, "You here again?" and a wry smile. I also had the pleasure of meeting Her Majesty the Queen and Prince Philip on the occasion of the 1978 festival. She had clearly been well briefed, saying, "Ah, you're playing the organ." The Royal Marines had a tradition of sending their directors of music to the RAM conductors' course for a year and Paul's successor, Graham Hoskins, was my contemporary on that course. It was good to work with him in Deal later, following Paul's retirement.

Over the years I have been something of a guest of the so-called session world – essentially a pool of freelance musicians who, for the most part, spend their lives travelling from studio to studio, having been engaged by specialist fixers to record music for film and television soundtracks, as well as 'jingles' for television and radio-station idents (identification tunes). For many years, a large number of those jingles have been written by Paul Hart, a viola player in the RYO. Our history goes back many years, as our mothers were both at school together in Seven Kings. Another beneficiary of musical life in Redbridge, Paul spent many years touring the world as an accompanist and jazz violinist with John Dankworth and Cleo Laine. He has worked extensively in music for films and television as well as writing many concert works. Apart from the piano and violin, his talents extend to playing many other instruments including the double bass and viola.

The first jingle we worked on together was for Hellman's mayonnaise, at the old CTS Studios – the concept being that whenever Hellman's was on-screen, I would play a very 'straight' version of Beethoven's *Für Elise*. When other brands were 'referenced', the style turned to a rather less conventional version played by Paul. We worked on quite a few interesting ads over the years, a couple of which involved me making quite a bit of noise on a loud pipe organ. Paul made a few appearances on *Friday Night,* and I know that the BBC would have liked him to do more, but he was far too busy to commit.

There were a couple of films that I particularly enjoyed working on, the first being *Dangerous Liaisons* (1989) starring Glenn Close. The music was recorded in a very short space of time in Abbey Road Studio 2 (the

A pub lunch with Leslie Pearson & Alistair Young (December 2015)

'Beatles' studio). This was the first time that I met the composer George Fenton, an inspiring and gentle man with whom I have worked on a number of occasions. The small orchestra was led by Gavyn Wright, and Catherine Bott was singing the soprano solos. The ongoing musical features of the film were specially arranged sections of Bach's Concerto in A minor for Four Harpsichords, for which I was joined by Leslie Pearson, John Toll and Guy Dagul. The harpsichords were supplied by Maurice Cochrane, who caused much amusement by running around during playbacks, valiantly trying to keep the four instruments not only in tune with themselves but also with the orchestra!

The other bit of fun came barely five minutes from the end of the session; after that, overtime is payable, which, of course, is to be avoided at all costs! Not for the first time in such a situation, the production team decided that we had just enough time to record the whole of the Allegro movement from which our extracts had been taken. I think all our minds were highly focused, as we were very aware that there were sections of this score which we had never played – also that there would be no opportunity to go back and make corrections.

Early in 1993, I had a call from George Fenton to ask whether I could give him some help for a forthcoming film, *Shadowlands*, starring Anthony Hopkins and Debra Winger. This moving film is based on the true story of an autumnal romance involving the British writer C.S. Lewis and a divorced American woman named Joy Gresham. Music was needed to accompany the shooting of the opening scene. In order to do this, they needed to produce a mock-up of the music that would be used, which would involve a small group of singers and my specialist organ samples. Ordinarily, the recording of a film score is the last aspect to be done, when everything else is edited and in place. However, this scene had specific requirements involving the procession of the choir into the chapel of Magdalen College, Oxford, for which George was writing a special piece of music based on the words *Veni Sancte Spiritus*.

I had a slight complication in that I was committed to an evening concert with the London Mozart Players in London's Queen Elizabeth Hall, and the recording was due to take place at the Twickenham Studios, the base of the genius sound engineer Keith Grant (affectionately known as Big Daddy). "No problem," said George, and they arranged a car to drive me back to the concert after I was set up. They made the basic recording of the vocal parts while I was away and the car drove me straight back to the studio after the concert. By the time I reached Twickenham it was quite late in the evening, and they were ready for me. What I wasn't prepared for was the presence of Lord Richard Attenborough (the producer, whose third collaboration this was with George Fenton) and also Debra Winger (the young American divorcee). That evening remains one of my most treasured memories. We worked until late into the night, adding the necessary organ sounds. The final track, as it appears on the film, was rerecorded by the choir and organ in the chapel of Magdalen College and is extraordinarily moving. I find this a very powerful piece of music and a reminder of that incredible preparatory evening. If you've not seen the film, I urge you to do so.

Some seven years later, this opening piece of music from *Shadowlands* was included in the special 1999 Prom *100 Years of Film Music*, mentioned earlier, with the BBCCO and George conducting. Walking towards the dressing room after the performance, I noticed the unmistakable figure of Lord Attenborough heading towards me (he was presenting the Prom). I was hugely touched when he looked straight at me and without any hesitation said, "Lovely to see you – that was a good evening in Twickenham," and went on his way.

As a postscript, Keith Grant was the driving force behind Olympic Studios which, in its day, was Britain's most successful independent recording studio and host to recordings by the likes of the Rolling

Stones, Led Zeppelin, the Beatles, the Jimi Hendrix Experience, The Eagles, BB King, Pink Floyd and David Bowie. In all, Keith personally recorded around 120 'Top 20' hits.

Back in the nineties, I joined Paul Hart for the two solo piano parts of *The Carnival of the Animals* with the RPO, outdoors at Crystal Palace. Somehow, they had managed to talk Keith into supervising the sound relay for the occasion. That was one of the rare occasions when I've heard an orchestra in a field actually sound like an orchestra! I've performed the The Carnival of the Animals twice with Alistair Young. The first being in the RAH (July 2004). The other being outdoors in Leicester Square (June 2006) with the RPO and conductor John Andrews. This was memorable for the hire company providing failing to provide any sustaining pedals with the electric pianos. This was resolved by the performance but it was a very uncomfortable rehearsal!

Whilst discussing adventures in film I should also mention, with some affection, being involved in many performances accompanying silent movies, with music composed and conducted by the renowned Carl Davis – an absolute master in that genre. *Ben Hur* and *Intolerance* particularly come to mind. Wonderful scores, but very long!

There has been a recent trend for the presenting of films with a 'live' orchestra playing the original soundtrack. These occasions currently generate large audiences which means that this is something of a growth industry. On these occasions, I can quite frequently be found sitting at a keyboard controlling a laptop that will produce not just fairly normal sounds, such as electric piano, harpsichord or organ, but also more adventurous sound effects such as for *Star Trek* and *Jurassic Park*.

The last occasion that I played the score for *Jurassic Park* was in Millennium Square, Leeds (2019). I worry that some people either don't research the suitability of films for young children, else they think that their children are special and can cope. This film is not about cuddly, pet-like dinosaurs – parts of it are seriously frightening. At this performance there were many young children, many of whom had to be carried out screaming. That being in stark contrast to the adult audience who, despite torrential rain, sat in their seats taking what the heavens were offering, as all good Brits do regularly at outdoor performances!

Recording the CD *English Oboe Concertos* with Ruth Bolister, Stephen Bell and the Elgar Chamber Orchestra (March 2003)

In 2001, my good friend Stephen Bell and the violinist, Lynette Wynn established the Elgar Chamber Orchestra, which gave several first-class public concerts. In 2003, the orchestra recorded a highly praised CD recording, *English Oboe Concertos*, with the oboist Ruth Bolister, whom I had previously met when she won the Isle of Wight International Oboe Competition in 1993. I had served for a number of years as a committee member alongside Lady Barbirolli, Norman Thurston and later, Nicholas Daniel. The recording was made in St Jude's Church, Hampstead Garden Suburb, but a rather smaller ensemble than assembled for many earlier recordings with the LSO. It was very cold, and we had to bring in extra lighting as well as infrared heaters. Although declaring an interest on this project as the producer, and also undertaking the subsequent mixing and post-production ahead of its release by ASV, I have to say the final result is superb and a great credit to Ruth, the orchestra and Steve.

Another career first arose one morning in September 2009 whilst I was walking across Ilford's Valentines Park – quite a common activity when heading towards the local station in those years. However, this occasion was somewhat eventful, as I received a call from someone telling me that he worked for the BBC's CBeebies channel and that he understood me to be a celeste soloist! Now, this is a title that I'd only previously encountered twice and, being something of a cynic when it comes to cold calls, I was rather cautious. I ran with it for a while and, after some further interaction, I established that CBeebies was piloting a new programme called *ZingZillas*. This turned out to be a musical, puppet-based programme with a curious obsession for coconuts. This particular episode was based on the idea of a broken music box, for which I was playing lots of tinkly sounds, including a performance of Liadov's *The Music Box* (they insisted on something that was non-copyright to keep down costs). This broadcast resulted in a fair bit of good-natured teasing from friends and colleagues who had been innocently watching the programme with their children! I was in very good company and other artists to have appeared in the series included Dame Evelyn Glennie, Julian Lloyd Webber, Nicola Benedetti, Cleo Laine and Sir John Dankworth.

November 2016 brought a most unusual engagement. I was invited to play Boëllmann's Toccata (for organ) at the Royal Albert Hall. However, as so often with such invitations, there was a twist! This solo was to accompany a film presentation as part of the London Fashion Awards, the film being a celebration of 100 Years of *British Vogue*, referred to as the 'Vogue Moment'. To start with, I had to record the piece so that they knew how long the film should be. This we did following an evening performance of *Classical Spectacular*, as I was already in the hall. When I played this for real on the night, I had to be able to keep the music in step with the film. The company had assumed we would use a click – in effect, an in-ear metronome. However, I pointed out that due to the volume of the organ, this would not be practical. We therefore had to make a plan to incorporate 'punches and streamers' into the film, which I could see at the organ on a small monitor. Punches are on-screen flashing dots that act as a metronome, and streamers move across the screen to indicate when a significant moment will arrive.

Backstage on the day was a revelation, as you might imagine from all the paraphernalia of the fashion world. I was given a dressing room from which I was later evicted when Donatella Versace apparently wanted it! We spent the evening surrounded by some very interestingly dressed people, at least from the perspective of our world, but we were very well looked after. Jo (page-turner) and I were offered food and handed a phone with a connection to Just Eat – being told to order whatever we wanted. The 'Vogue Moment' went smoothly, and we were booked an Uber for our journey home.

Thinking about the technicalities of this production reminds me just how different the world of film was back in the mid-eighties when I started recording music for soundtracks. Playback of the film during recording was from 'reels', meaning that if we stopped for any reason, we had to wait for the projectionist to rewind to the start – this could take some time. These days, this is all digital and playback is instant from a computer hard drive, saving both time and money.

There have been many happy days working in studios with British composers such as Nigel Hess, Debbie Wiseman and Christopher Gunning who, in addition to his other work, is still writing wonderful symphonies – currently thirteen and counting, several of which I've had the pleasure of recording with him and the RPO. In addition to working on the strictly music side of films, I have, on a few occasions, strayed onto film sets into the world of film-making, such as playing dummy (non-sounding) piano for *Ellis Island* (1984 with Richard Burton and Faye Dunaway) and *Déjà Vu* (1985 with Jaclyn Smith, of *Charlie's Angels* fame).

There have also been some large-scale in-vision TV ads; notably, a couple of days at Clandon Park in fancy dress, recording a coffee advert by way of Bach's *Coffee Cantata*. Another occasion was for a new Sony Walkman that saw the whole of the old Alexandra Palace Theatre full of musicians, playing a multitude of keyboards and other instruments (October 2007). I was one of four playing a quartet of toy pianos. This was somewhat backbreaking, and every so often I felt compelled to stand for a moment, only to be yelled at by the floor manager to 'sit down'!

Sony Walkman • Lucy Morris, Dylan Bates, Claire Dibble (2007)

Sony Walkman • Alexandra Palace Theatre (2007)

16 – Ongar Music Club

In 1975, my dear friend, Geoffrey Timms, with whom I taught a little at the time for the London Borough of Redbridge at Beal Grammar (later High) School, mentioned to me that he, and some like-minded musical friends in the small market town of Ongar in Essex, were forming a music club. This proved to be a huge success, in no small measure due to the influence of another co-founder, Barrie Hall – a past publicity officer for Radio 3 – together with his wife, Jean. A larger-than-life character, Barrie knew everyone who was anyone and then a few more, and he somehow managed to cajole the likes of Yehudi Menuhin, Dame Eva Turner, Sir Peter Pears, Denis Matthews, Steven Isserlis and Richard Baker into appearing for Ongar Music Club for a very reasonable fee, if any.

I was invited to give a piano recital the following year, and from that time, my relationship with the club grew. In 1984, Geoffrey had the excellent idea of starting a yearly competition – to find the Essex Young Musician of the Year. John Lill has supported the competition since its inception and has allowed the awards to be in his name. This has run every year since (although sadly not 2020), and most of the winners have gone on to highly successful careers in the music profession. These have included the pianist Benjamin Grosvenor, violinist Anthony Marwood, pianist Joseph Tong and countertenor Timothy Wayne-Wright.

We celebrated the club's twenty-fifth anniversary in 2000 with a two-piano marathon, with funds being raised for the Ongar & District Community Association. There were ten of us, and we presented music,

Playing opposite the late Geoffrey Timms, as part of Ongar Music Club's charity two-piano marathon, Ongar (2000)

mostly in pairs, on two pianos. For the grand finale, we all played a new arrangement of the *Dance of the Little Swans* from Tchaikovsky's *Swan Lake* ballet made by a club member, John Harrop – ten hands per piano! Geoffrey Timms and I played Bach, Shostakovich and Rachmaninov.

With Mauro Sheehan and Geoffrey Timms, Ongar (July 2015)

The year 2015 was a particularly special one for the competition, when Geoffrey drove from his new home in North Wales to chair the panel of adjudicators. This was also a special occasion for Mauro Sheehan, a mutual star pupil, who came to join us for the meal break between the semi-final and final rounds. The competition continues to thrive, and occasionally we are joined by John Lill on the adjudication panel.

Although Ongar Music Club doesn't now present regular evening concerts, it does have a series of lunchtime recitals called *Soundbites!* – these incorporate afternoon tea and were the brainchild of the current chairman, the soprano Jane Webster. This is a very different idea from that originally conceived, but it does keep the club alive. We miss many of the founder members, some no longer with us, and others who gave long service on the club's committee and are now unable to stay in support for a variety of reasons – Nicola Harries, Peter Jackson and Janet Pope who, like many others, have given so much of their time for the club.

At some point in the early nineties, a lovely young lady named Joanna Smith appeared before the adjudicators in Ongar. She had a musicality and rhythmic drive about her playing that was captivating. We kept in touch, meeting for the annual competition, which she was either entering as a pianist or, later, as an accompanying pianist. Jo would write me a long letter every Christmas that I looked forward to receiving, although it wasn't until a good few years later that we actually met up for a meal and some piano-duet playing. The rest is history, and Ongar Music Club will always hold a special place in our hearts.

I can't leave my previous reference to Beal High School without mention of the headmaster, John Manuel, who was amazingly supportive and proud of the school's excellent music tradition, under the direction of Geoffrey Timms. Although a historian, John had been a choral scholar at Cambridge and had a fine voice. He regularly featured as a soloist in his school's musical productions as well as other concerts in the local area. He was also exceedingly supportive when it came to my being released from teaching commitments – on one occasion, for three weeks to go on tour with the BBCSO. One of his greatest ambitions was for his school to present a concert on London's South Bank, and this he did in March 1983 to a capacity audience in the Queen Elizabeth Hall, with an ambitious programme that included *Hiawatha's Wedding Feast*. The choir at that time was of a remarkable standard, and comprised not just pupils (or had they by then been upgraded to students?) but also staff, a number of whom sang regularly in the choir of St Edward the Confessor in Romford with Jonathan Venner. Geoffrey Timms worked like a Trojan to put this event together and was assisted on the occasion by another member of staff, Peter Stannard. The programme included Handel's Organ Concerto Op. 4 No. 5, for which I joined the assembled company. The other soloist was a friend of John Manuel, the operatic tenor, Geoffrey Pogson.

Beal High School charity gala concert • Queen Elizabeth Hall (March 1983)

17 – Writing and Recording

I've always enjoyed writing music and remember a very early piano piece I wrote for a competition at school (CLS) called *The Seasons* – hardly an original concept, but I didn't know that back then and would probably cringe to hear it now. Later, I wrote quite a few choir and organ pieces for church performances during my time as organist at Gants Hill URC. Some of these involved an orchestra, such as a setting of the Te Deum and a somewhat quirky arrangement of 'O Come, All Ye Faithful' with an orchestral introduction in 7/8 – this always caused amusement (and rehearsal difficulties!), but the idea may have been a hint of things to come.

By good fortune, we had a very fine flautist in our church choir – Carolyn Wheadon (née Taylor). At some point in the early nineties, my assistant organist suggested I might make an arrangement or two for the annual Service of Nine Lessons and Carols to incorporate the flute. The next day, with one of those very rare (for me, anyway) moments of inspiration, I sat down and wrote my arrangement of 'Gabriel's Message'. This was closely followed by 'Rocking' and 'Angels From the Realms of Glory'. A friend with contacts in the world of publishing was aware of my endeavours and put out some feelers for me, eventually leading to my making contact with Andrew Skirrow at Camden Music. This set of carols was published under the title of *Three Carols* – they did very well, and some commissions started to arrive. Almost immediately I realised that I would need to add orchestrations to broaden their accessibility and went ahead with those, keeping to a relatively small orchestra in order to give maximum playability for a variety of ensemble requirements.

In general, all my carol arrangements are for strings with wind quintet plus a couple of percussionists, together with harp and celeste, both of which, if needs be, can be played by electronic keyboard instruments or piano. Flexibility has always seemed an important consideration to me. Many other carol arrangements followed, together with some original settings and versions for high voices. I have always appreciated the support of Raymond Gubbay Ltd, and they have regularly programmed my music in their annual Christmas Festival, as well as commissioning my arrangements of 'Rudolph the Red-Nosed Reindeer' and 'We Three

Kings' which was written for a Barbican performance given by the choir of St George's Chapel, Windsor with the English Chamber Orchestra.

My friend Jonathan Venner has been organist and director of music at the church of St Edward the Confessor in Romford for well over forty years now. In that time we have been through many musical adventures together – making music in Romford, and also during cathedral visits with the choir, singing the daily services and sometimes playing the organ. Jonathan has always been hugely supportive of my writing, and along the way, we have made numerous recordings together. The album *Magnificat!* (2000) involved all the parish choirs and the Wykeham Sinfonia, an orchestra drawn largely from professional musicians living in the area surrounding Romford. The repertoire included John Rutter's glittering setting of the Magnificat, featuring our good friend, the soprano Julia Wilson-James. Jonathan also included many of my carol arrangements in their versions for SATB and orchestra. This was a very happy but tiring day during which we recorded a great deal of music. We would have run out of time had it not been for the remarkable diplomacy and enthusiasm of the co-leader, Keith Gurry, who encouraged the assembled players to give us an extra fifteen minutes of recording time without charge, in order to finish. That generosity of spirit was hugely appreciated.

Keith Gurry was a very special person and a wonderful violinist, and we had been friends for more years than I can remember. After studies

Jonathan Venner directing the Wykeham Sinfonia and the choirs of St Edward's Church Romford in the recording of the CD *Magnificat*. Our good friends Nat Paris (Orchestra of the Royal Opera House) playing double bass and Keith Gurry (BBCSO) on the front desk of first violins (2000)

Massed choirs joining for the recording of Martin Neary's newly commissioned anthem *O Worship the Lord* (2000)

at the RAM he joined the RPO, although a little too early for our paths to have crossed. He served on the board of directors for some time before leaving the orchestra to join the BBCSO, where we met many times in the eighties. Keith would be a familiar figure to anyone who watched the *Last Night of the Proms* in those days, sitting in the second violins, just in front of the conductor.

Keith lived close by in his family home in Wanstead, and we would infrequently meet for a meal, most usually in one of his favourite local Indian or Chinese restaurants. Eating, like playing the violin, was a great pleasure for Keith! One of his regular tricks, having ordered the meal, was to call the waiter back and whisper in his ear in hushed tones, accompanied by a wink across the table – I knew that soon some extra dishes would arrive on the table! The last time I saw Keith was the occasion of my sixtieth birthday meal at Luigi's restaurant in Gants Hill, a favourite haunt for years and rather conveniently situated at the end of our road. There was some doubt as to whether Keith would come – he had been very low following the theft of his treasured violins from the doorstep of his home whilst letting himself in one evening. However, he came, sat at our 'top table' and moved me beyond measure with a totally impromptu speech for the occasion.

Keith's funeral took place at the City of London Crematorium on 14th June 2012, and I was privileged to play the organ for the service. This was an emotional occasion – the chapel was full to capacity with friends, colleagues and members of the BBCSO, all wanting to show their respect and love for one of the much loved *gentlemen* of the profession.

There's a lovely anecdote from 1992 when we gave a performance at St Edward's of Bernstein's *Chichester Psalms*. This was the chamber version, for which I was joined by colleagues from the LPO: harpist Rachel Masters and percussionist Russell Jordan (actually the LPO's timpanist). At the time Jonathan had a very fine organ student, Stuart Nicholson, destined for great things, whom Jonathan had asked to turn my pages and also make some stop changes for me, due to the lack of playing aids on the St Edward's organ. With characteristically thorough preparation, Stuart was seen one morning in the organ loft, listening to a recording of the work and rehearsing the stop changes and page turns!

In 2003, the choristers, together with Jonathan Venner, Stuart Nicholson (keyboards) and Carolyn Wheadon (flute) made a delightful recording of my complete high voice carol arrangements for the CD *In Dulci Jubilo*. I have always valued the support and encouragement offered by Jonathan, not to mention considerable practical advice from someone who spends his life putting into practice what the likes of me think we've written!

Jo with Keith Gurry, Mary Spiers and George Pig at my 60th Birthday celebration • Keith admiring the main course! • Luigi's restaurant, Gants Hill (October 2011)

Recording the CD *A Little Fall-ish!* in Temple Church • (bottom left) Martin Owen and Andrew Nicholson considering some finer details (August 2005)

I was soon busy exploring other instrumental genres, realising, before long, that I had enough material for a CD. This first release was recorded in August 2005 in the delightful surroundings of Temple Church in London which, with my history in the building from school days, was like stepping back in time. The orchestra was the RPO and the conductor, Stephen Bell (now associate conductor, Hallé Pops). As I mentioned, Steve and I have been good friends for a good many years since his time as principal horn of the BBCCO – another conductor whose musical experience comes very much from inside the orchestra.

We were made very welcome at Temple Church by the verger, Brian Nicholson, whom I knew through his son, Stuart Nicholson – he really couldn't do enough to help. Although stunningly beautiful, the building also had its challenges. The only realistic place to fit an orchestra, albeit a smallish one, was in what is known as the Round. However, in this area, the reverberation, whilst appealing, was far too long for our purposes, so we brought in some very high black drapes that we flew across the middle of the space. Of course, there was no way of knowing whether we had judged it correctly, but in practice the acoustic was damped just enough to be controlled, and we were all delighted with the results.

The two days of recording included my Concertino for Celeste and Chamber Orchestra, *Four Seasonal Nocturnes*, *Cygncopations*, *Paean* and a couple of miniatures for piano and orchestra. On the third day, I also recorded my *Twelve Astrological Preludes* for piano. Although these were originally planned for inclusion on this album, in the event the CD was completed with a recording of my suite *Back to Bach* that was made with the RPO in the following summer. The piano preludes would have to wait another few years to see the light of day. I was delighted that the greatly respected Mike Dutton released this CD on his Dutton-Epoch label under the title *A Little Fall-ish!*

I was already planning a second album with the RPO to record some of my Christmas repertoire with orchestra. We booked a session at St John's, Smith Square in July 2006 to record *Back to Bach*, in order to complete the previous CD, as well as *Fanfare da Festa* and the suite for organ and orchestra, *Wassailing Down the Wind,* for the new album. These two pieces we recorded without using the Smith Square organ, as I felt the instrument in Temple Church would be better suited to the music. We returned to Temple Church in May 2007 to 'overdub' the missing sections.

Now I had to make a decision about which choir would join us for the new Christmas recording and, after much discussion, it seemed

Recording *Festive Frolic*, St John's, Smith Square (Feb. 2007)

Stephen Bell with harpist Suzy Willison-Kawalec.

Playback with Stephen Bell and engineer David Wright.

Stephen Quigley discussing my percussion writing!

that the obvious option was to invite Peter Broadbent and his Joyful Company of Singers. That was a decision that I never regretted – they were prepared by Peter with considerable care, and their performances in the recording sessions (February 2007) were exemplary and delivered with good humour and enthusiasm.

The conductor on this recording was, once again, Stephen Bell. The keyboard parts were played by Alistair Young, who did a wonderful job in the very challenging circumstances of having a piano and chamber organ on the stage, and everyone else much further down on the floor of the hall. Jo (my fiancée at the time) also joined us for the title track *Festive Frolic,* which has a part for synthesizer.

Festive Frolic had actually been commissioned by the London Borough of Redbridge for its fortieth biennial choral festival in the RAH in 2006. For many years, from 1976, I had played the organ for this special occasion. The new piece (on that occasion called *Festival Frolic*) is dedicated to Malcolm Bidgood, and I was invited to conduct it for that first performance. It was then that I developed a greater sympathy for those conductors who, over the years, had complained bitterly about the sensation of conducting choirs in that hall at the end of an elastic band!

There were challenges following the recording sessions for *Festive Frolic* due to our forthcoming wedding on Easter Day 2007 (8th April), and certain aspects of the CD production had to be put on hold. I was very keen to start editing the recordings, but I had to keep a grip on reality so as not to compromise our domestic plans, whilst also being mindful of not missing the sign-off deadline for Naxos in the early summer.

In 2008, Jo and I travelled to Atlanta for the US premiere of my Christmas suite for organ and orchestra, *Wassail Down the Wind*. This took place in the generously proportioned and hugely impressive Peachtree Road United Methodist Church, and the event marked the first concert performance using the new Gallery Organ by Manders – this being in

Conducting *Festival Frolic*, RAH (2006)

With Jo, Nicole Marane and John Mander (December 2008)

addition to the substantial Mander installation at the east end! It was a pleasure to catch up with John Mander at that special concert – John had also been at CLS. This was a remarkably festive occasion in which the main organ was played by Nicole Marane, the conductor being the church's director of music, Scott Atchison. On the same trip, I also caught up for drinks with my friend John Scott. By this time, Jo was suffering somewhat from the trials of pregnancy, which prevented her from joining us. However, this didn't stop us from meeting our American friends Rebecca (also expecting) and Mike for an extravagant meal in New York's famous The River Café, situated in the shadow of the Brooklyn Bridge.

Since leaving the RCM, Jo had worked regularly with The Aurora Ensemble – a fine wind quintet under the leadership of clarinettist Andrew Mason. I had previously written a short encore piece for some of the group called *Funky Fugato,* and in 2011 I expanded that, adding parts for flute and horn. I seemed to be getting away with this, so I continued with what grew to be a twenty-five-minute piano and wind sextet named *Moody Moves.* This we recorded in Henry Wood Hall across a weekend in early January 2012, along with the new versions of my two cor anglais pieces, *Cygncopations* and *Il Cygnet,* played by the eminent saxophonist Kyle Horch in partnership with my wife.

On the following Monday I headed to Brentwood Cathedral with my friend and recording partner-in-crime David Wright (a wizard when it comes to all matters sonic), and we set up to record my *Two Anglo Fandangos* for guitar and organ and *Two Festive Carillons* for organ. David and I have worked together on many recordings over the years, and it's so reassuring that we have such a similar approach to achieving a good sound. Once again the organist was Stuart Nicholson, currently director of music at St Patrick's Cathedral in Dublin – the guitarist was his wife, Victoria Green. *Moody Moves* was the title for this new CD issued by Herald, which also contained the complete recording of *Twelve Astrological Preludes* that I had recorded in Temple Church back in the summer of 2005.

Kyle Horch with David Wright recording *Cygncopations* (2012)

The Aurora Ensemble recording *Moody Moves* (2012)

The first of the *Two Anglo Fandangos* had actually been written for Victoria and Stuart as a wedding present back in 2002 (I think it may have been late!). I knew nothing about the guitar then, and little more now. I persevered with some help from Google and other such sources, and at least managed to discover that it was a transposing instrument! However, I retained a sense of insecurity about the whole process and certainly didn't want to offer the couple something that would be unplayable! Life stepped in again … I had recently been asked to take on an organ-playing engagement for which, apparently, all the details were cloaked in secrecy. All I knew was that there was a reasonably generous fee and that I had to get a particular flight one morning from London Heathrow. Even so, I decided that no matter what the fee, I wasn't setting foot on a plane without being able to tell my family where I was going – we reached something of an impasse! During the course of that day, I became aware of a certain amount of razzmatazz in the press about a forthcoming celebrity wedding to be held in a small town in Ireland. I asked whether they could deny that this was connected, which they couldn't, so I decided to go ahead! I had been told that I didn't need to take any music with me, just a suit.

So it was that I found myself walking down the aisle of a plane bound for Belfast, looking forward to tucking into the four-star breakfast that would no doubt be forthcoming from British Midland. Duly seated, I was then astounded to be joined in the next seat by none other than Carlos Bonell, the celebrated guitarist with whom I had previously worked for Radio 2. It transpired that he was on the same musical mystery tour as me. Without too much delay, I pulled out the score of my new piece (*Fandango Fantástico*) and handed it to Carlos with a red pen for his comments! Advice was offered most graciously, and I was rather chuffed that apart from simplifying a few chords and lowering some particularly high notes, he gave it a clean bill of health.

The next few days were great fun. We stayed in Jury's Inn in Belfast, and the assembled company also included trumpeters Maurice Murphy and Paul Archibald. We had some enjoyable breakfasts in the famous Crown pub (which has the distinction of being Belfast's most-bombed pub) and travelled by coach to the church for rehearsals and, ultimately, the wedding. I asked the music director whether I needed any music in addition to what he had supplied. "No," was the reply – I wasn't so sure! With a growing sense of unease, I found a music shop in Belfast to buy some suitable music to cover me against unexpected emergencies. In the event, the church was full forty-five minutes before the scheduled start of the service, and then the bride was late by much the same length of time, so I was glad of the investment! Whilst I'm happy to improvise, I think that an hour and a half might have proved to be a challenge.

Meanwhile, I was growing increasingly uncomfortable about the fact that I'd not seen any hymn books, either in the body of the church or, more curiously, on the organ. I queried this and was told that the words would be on the Order of Service – not especially helpful to the organist. Whilst all the hymns were extremely well known, I felt that in this situation, with no doubt a very musical and elite congregation, now was not the time for a memory test. Once back in Belfast, I messaged Jonathan Venner to ask whether he could help with some music, and his wife Deborah kindly faxed the hymns to the hotel – this felt like a lifeline. The same evening I discovered the likely reason for the absence of any hymn book on the organ console, which is something I've never previously encountered in a functioning church. I was in my hotel room watching Sky News,

which was running a feature on the impending nuptials and showing the crowds in the town that had gathered in anticipation. They went into the local pub to interview the publican, and he was asked about there being a family

With Maurice Murphy, Carlos Bonell and Paul Archibald.

connection with the church that was hosting the wedding. "Yes," he said, "my wife is the organist, but she's not been asked to play." I think we know where the organist's hymn book went! Apart from my impromptu organ recital, all went smoothly and we were treated to the first part of the reception on the lawn outside – very picturesque and a unique experience.

In 2010, I set about revisiting my recording of organ music by Percy Whitlock, which had been released on the respected Libra Realsound cassette label back in 1985. This had been recorded on the organ of Rugby School Chapel, which was well suited to this romantic repertoire. My friend Peter Bullett was, at the time, head of physics at Rugby and had suggested the organ might suit the project. He was keen to help with the practicalities, which also involved the onerous task of page-turning. David Wright, who ran this cassette label, joined us in Rugby, and Peter and his wife Alison were our hosts for the nights that we stayed there. My biggest challenge was that of staying awake. Due to traffic noise from the one-way system outside the chapel, we had to start recording very late in the evening, working into the early hours – something I've always found difficult.

David and I were both very fond of this digital recording and decided it would be good to release it as a CD so that its full quality could be appreciated. However, we were short of material as the length required for a cassette was substantially less than for a CD. Another issue arose for recording more music – the old organ in Rugby School Chapel had long since been replaced by a splendid new instrument, but one that was not stylistically suited to the music or compatible with what we had already recorded. The solution proved to be very close to home – the lovely romantic instrument in Brentwood

Rugby School Chapel • Organ console behind the lectern (1985)

Premiere of *Pipe Dream* with Ellie and Richard (2018)

Cathedral – a building with which I already had a very good relationship. The master of the music, Andrew Wright, and his assistant, Margaret MacLeay, were only too willing to help. Andrew is also a hugely gifted composer and arranger, and I've joined him for a good many cathedral recordings, acting as producer. When it came to recording the extra pieces, Whitlock's *Sortie* from the *Seven Sketches* and the magnificent Fantasie Chorale No. 2 in F sharp minor, I had a streaming cold, but somehow we struggled through, and it all came together really well. The new album was released by Herald under the title *The Gentle Art of Percy Whitlock*. The design on the CD cover was painted specially for the album by Colin Foo, who also helped with aspects of this book's dust jacket.

It was a chance meeting in July 2016 with the trumpet player Ellie Lovegrove, and our ensuing conversation about repertoire for trumpet and organ, that broadly gave rise to my next album, *A Windy Christmas*. I had always enjoyed this medium and discovering that Ellie had an established partnership (*Illumina Duo*) with the organist Richard Moore (sub-organist at Guildford Cathedral), I was encouraged to make a start on a new writing project. This led to the writing of *Pipe Dream* (2018) for trumpet and organ, which was followed fairly swiftly by *Advent Dances* (2019), inspired by the grand advent hymn tune, *Veni Emmanuel*. Ellie and Richard brought a great sense of fun and enthusiasm to the writing of these pieces, for which I am very grateful.

In the meantime, Jonathan Venner had also commissioned some new carol arrangements with brass quintet for his lunchtime Christmas carol service at Romford. This inspired *Deck the Hall*, which was swiftly followed by *Past Three O'Clock* and the wonderfully haunting *Wexford Carol*. As these progressed, it seemed that each was in roughly the style of a baroque dance and they were therefore published under the title *Three 'Baroque' Carols*. These are now orchestrated, and in December 2019 the Royal Liverpool Philharmonic Orchestra and Chorus gave the first performance of *Deck the Hall* in this version, conducted by Ian Tracey. I had also written other instrumental wind music for the festive season – *A Windy Christmas* for wind or brass quintet and *Christmas Mudley*, which has now been arranged for almost every conceivable combination of instruments (most recently for brass quintet). I soon realised that, together with my Christmas organ solo *A Christmas Carillon*, I was close to having enough music for a new album, and that this could be not only festive but also wind-based. I also had *Two Michaelmas Carol Anthems*, both with an *obbligato* oboe part, and I invited my esteemed friend and colleague John Anderson to play for these. I also wrote him a new piece, *Sails at Dawn*, based on the carol *I Saw Three Ships*, as well as reworking my full orchestral arrangement of *Rudolph the Red-Nosed Reindeer* for oboe and piano. Both of these John recorded, with my wife Jo playing the piano.

We recorded in February 2019 at Henry Wood Hall. Once again I invited my friend Peter Broadbent and his Joyful Company of Singers for choral support, Chaconne Brass to record the pieces with brass quintet and The Aurora Ensemble to record *A Windy Christmas* as well as a new piece, *Holly's Nightmare*, which is based on *The Holly and the Ivy*. I also made a special arrangement of *Merry Gents* from the suite *Wassailing in the Dark* for The Aurora Ensemble and organ (actually far from merry, rather more lugubrious and marked *poco intoxicato*). As is probably clear by now, I take some delight in choosing the right titles and score markings! For the trumpet and organ aspects on this new album, we once again returned to the inspiring surroundings, organ and acoustic of Brentwood Cathedral.

As may be clear, Christmas writing has become something of a year-round occupation for me, and I was very touched that in 2017, John Rutter included my Christmas piece *Noel!* for organ and orchestra in his Christmas

Master choral director, Peter Broadbent • Henry Wood Hall (2019)

concerts with the RPO. The solo organ part was played by Andrew Lucas in the RAH and Jonathan Scott in Manchester's Bridgewater Hall.

It so happened that whilst I was writing *Advent Dances* (for trumpet and organ) our nine-year-old son, Matthew, was working alongside me in the studio. He became very excited about a variation that was in the style of a gigue, and would dance around the house singing it – this section became *Matty's Gigue*! He later memorised the whole trumpet part as it developed, leading to such an interest in the instrument that we bought him a cornet for Christmas and lessons began. At the time of writing, he has also become very keen on arranging and typesetting music, as well as preparing for theory exams, taking one per term until the present pandemic prevented this. He also wants to learn the horn and oboe – plenty of ambition. Matthew is obviously growing up in a musical household, and he made his first foreign trip with us at the age of five months when I was playing *The Carnival of the Animals* in Jersey with the RPO.

I've been asked what it's like the first time you hear your music played. In fact, it's not so much hearing the music, as you obviously know what your expectations are. Even so, it's always a real treat to hear your music played by real musicians with the flexibility that this affords rather than an unemotional computer. For me, the first play-through is more an anxiety as to whether the instrumental or vocal parts are correct or, at a more personal level, whether colleagues will appreciate what you've written or give you a slow handclap! After all, the hope is to create something that others will enjoy performing and listening to. I remember discussing this

Matthew playing carols with the Rayleigh Training Band (2019)

this with the renowned arranger and composer Gordon Langford, a regular contributor to BBCCO programmes. He told me that on many occasions he'd been so anxious that he wanted to wait outside until the first play-through was finished – hopefully without incident.

I suppose that for anyone there's always an element of needing to know that your work is appreciated and accepted. It's therefore been reassuring to receive positive feedback and encouragement, by way of many enthusiastic reviews in this country as well as in other countries such as North America and Australia.

Since the mid-nineties my music has been published by Andrew Skirrow at Camden Music, and he has been very supportive in making my catalogue widely available through the distributor, Spartan Press. Camden Music also came up with a very attractive design for the covers. They also handle all my hire library.

I'm very aware that, over the years, I have been privileged to be surrounded by very patient orchestral friends and colleagues, always willing to give a moment of their time to advise on any queries regarding playability! I'm particularly indebted to Suzy Willison-Kawalec and Stephen Quigley from the RPO.

Recording the CD *A Windy Christmas* with Bramwell Tovey, the Joyful Company of Singers and Chaconne Brass • Henry Wood Hall (2019)

18 – Family

I spent the evening of the millennium in the Royal Albert Hall with the BBCCO. The hall had been booked years earlier by Raymond Gubbay, who never missed a trick. We gave two patriotically based concerts, as only Gubbay's can do, and the backstage bar became party central! We finished the second concert at around 10:00pm, when I drove to Collier Row to see in the New Year with my friends Jonathan and Deborah Venner, having first called in on Mum and Dad in Gants Hill to wish them well. Even before midnight, I remember seeing the sky periodically ablaze with the fireworks of over-zealous celebrants!

My parents had not long since celebrated their golden wedding anniversary (May 1999), which was a fairly low-key affair at home. Mum didn't want a fuss or any sort of party – I think they were both finding such occasions to be increasingly challenging, not least because of Dad's declining health. He had suffered from emphysema for many years as a direct result of smoking, and more recently he had developed a tumour. The last time they came out to hear me play was early in 2001 for a special performance of Beethoven's *Choral Fantasy*. Dad was determined to be there, albeit with an oxygen cylinder.

He was admitted to hospital a few days before Easter that year when his breathing deteriorated quite drastically one evening. This was obviously a difficult time, but only once did Mum ask whether I thought Dad would pull through.

I took Mum to see him in Oldchurch Hospital on the afternoon before he passed away and he was typically stoic – saying he was going to fight it and telling us what the medics were going to do to help him. I remember looking back and seeing him beaming as we left – we didn't see each other again. Later that evening he rang to talk to Mum and, as I

Mum and Dad's Golden Wedding Anniversary (1999)

had been staying with her since he was hospitalised, he asked to speak to me. His last words were, "Look after Mum." I'm sure he knew …

Dad passed away that night, in the early hours of St George's Day. He was a great patriot, in the nicest sense of the word, and I value being able to think of him on that special day each year. It has always been a particular sadness that Dad never knew Jo and Matthew. Although he would have seen her playing the piano at the Essex Young Musician of the Year competition in Ongar, he would not have thought anything of it other than to appreciate her playing – he wouldn't have known what was to be.

I eventually decided it was time to move back home (actually just round the corner from my parents' home), although I felt as though I was abandoning Mum after what had been quite a lengthy stay. The following years had their challenges. Mum had become quite frail and suffered a few falls, resulting in several stays in hospital. Despite her difficulties, she did manage to get to our wedding at Holy Trinity Church, Southchurch, supported by her close friend Pat Flood who, together with her husband Derek, gave up their Easter Day to help.

We were wonderfully supported by friends, many of whom formed a choir, conducted by Malcolm Hicks, to sing, amongst other things, Mascagni's *Easter Hymn* from *Cavalleria Rusticana* – what a splendid piece to be able to include on Easter Day! The organ was, of course, played

Our musician friends who played in the service • Martin Owen, Elizabeth Burley, Leslie Pearson, Martin Hurrell, Stephen Quigley, Alistair Young, Helen Shillito, Andrew Mason, Peter Bullett and Stephen Bell (not pictured) (April 2007)

by Peter Bullett and the other organ (yes, there are two in Holy Trinity) was played by Alistair Young. Julia Wilson-James sang Quilter's *Love's Philosophy* accompanied by Elizabeth Burley, and there were readings from Jonathan Venner and Jo's mum, Liz. We lit the Easter candle in memory of Dad – how he would have loved this occasion, and I like to think that at some level he may have been able to appreciate it. Jo looked stunning – her sister-in-law, Karen, was her bridesmaid; her brothers, Phil and Jef, together with Alistair Young, were ushers and I was hugely supported throughout the day by my best man – Bramwell Tovey.

We had a lovely reception at The Lawn in Rochford, at which I was warmly welcomed into my wife's family by Jo's father, Alan. The weather was unseasonably sunny and warm. Emma Ramsdale played the harp, a quartet of friends played for us during the meal, and a small band played some traditional light and jazz numbers during the evening reception, which Lindsay Benson joined as vocalist – Lindsay and I had shared the same primary school back in the 1950s as well as the RAM.

Did I have a stag night? Well yes, but not in the conventional sense. Martin Owen had narrowed down a few possible central-London venues for such an occasion, and together we spent a happy few hours researching them. Eventually we settled on Floridita – a lively Cuban dinner/dance venue in Wardour Street with a terrific salsa atmosphere. Jo and I actually had a semi-combined stag and hen night with two large tables set next to each other. So far as I'm aware, nothing untoward occurred, although I admit that towards the end I may not have been totally aware of all that was happening, particularly in respect of what was being put in my glass!

The years after Dad passed away were very precious. I lived at the other end of the estate where Mum was living in Tillotson Road and most evenings when at home, I would walk round and spend a little time with her. Sometimes I would cross paths with

Our reception quartet – Keith Gurry, Lorraine Kelly, Elisa Bergerson and Becky Cox (April 2007)

Our reception 'band' – Simon Ashford, Dave Allaway, Nat Paris, John Malam, Mike Kitts and Lindsay Benson (April 2007)

Gaurika, the very musically talented daughter of our near neighbour Biri Sangha, himself a published writer. We would stop for a chat, and I'm delighted to know that she is now doing great things in the 'pop' side of our business.

Mum became very poorly in 2008 and was taken into hospital while Jo and I were on holiday in the Canaries. The advice was that she was comfortable and that we shouldn't interrupt our short holiday, during which we were in constant touch on her situation. When we returned, we discovered that Mum had lost a great deal of weight; she was very weak, and I was given her grave diagnosis, which we didn't share with her.

This was a very difficult time at home – Jo was hugely supportive at a time when I was pretty much planning Mum's funeral. Therefore the news that she had started to put on weight came as a big surprise, and she was eventually admitted to Springfield Care Home in Barkingside. After many questions and investigations, her consultant gave me a written, unreserved apology for the distress caused by an incorrect diagnosis. Springfield Care Home was to be Mum's home for the rest of her life.

June 2009 heralded the arrival of our wonderful son, Matthew. This also brought great joy to Mum, and she did manage to venture out for his christening. This was held a week before Christmas that year, and her presence brought a special dimension to the service, which was conducted by my late uncle, the Reverend Colin Nowell, a minister all his life.

Mum was also joined by her lifelong friend Lily, whom she met in the Ilford Maternity Hospital whilst Lily and her late husband, Norman, were awaiting the arrival of their daughter Lorraine. Lily and Norman had remained close friends with my parents, sharing many holidays. My parents greatly valued their friends and family. In addition to their UK friends, they had also met Bea and Charlie from Miami, while on holiday in Jamaica – a lovely couple with whom they stayed many times, both in the US and Ilford.

For the most part, Mum enjoyed a comfortable time in Springfield. I managed to visit most days whilst still living at Gants Hill but, of necessity, visits became a little less frequent following our move to Thundersley. The presence of Matthew on some visits brought a smile to Mum's face, which I otherwise didn't frequently see.

One morning in February 2016, Mum was taken into King George Hospital after a bad coughing fit, though things had calmed by lunchtime. I was working but told not to go to the hospital with any sense of urgency as she was now sitting up, eating lunch and looking comfortable. In retrospect, I wish I had, but I made the decision, which Mum would probably have approved of, to go to Croydon for a performance of Mussorgsky's *Pictures at an Exhibition*. I received a call from the hospital during *Gnomes* to tell me I should go to the hospital at once. I was excused duty and made the drive from Croydon to Goodmayes in the rush hour – I hope never to have to make such a challenging journey again. Sadly, I was too late.

Matthew's christening with Mum, the Reverend (Uncle) Colin and Mum's lifelong friend, Lily Hobley (December 2009)

Matthew with Grandma Hazel, Bethell Avenue (2009)

Matthew's 7th birthday celebrations (2016)

Matthew following in Daddy's footsteps and having a little tootle in the Royal Albert Hall (July 2015)

19 – Coda

I've frequently been asked what sort of music I like to listen to outside of 'classical music'. In practice, I tend to listen more to talk radio than music, but maybe that's not so surprising when spending much of my life surrounded by music. I grew up at secondary school in the age of the Beatles and small groups of us at school would make attempts to reproduce their music – in reality it wasn't that complicated though, of course, it sounded nothing like them! Although rather carried along with the general euphoria of the time, I've never 'got' the screaming that accompanies so much of the pop era. It reminds me of certain concerts in which we sometimes play music written for video games. I only have to play the first couple of delicate piano notes from, say, *Angry Birds* and the hall erupts, totally obscuring any music for quite a while.

I enjoyed much of the classic rock genre, and in the late-seventies and eighties, I would often listen to a mix of Sade, Linda Ronstadt (with that master arranger, Nelson Riddle and his orchestra) and later, Diana Krall. A particularly favourite album from that time was *Why Not?* by the amazing Michel Camilo, and for something completely different, and with a glass of something warming in my hand, it had to be Enya's *Watermark!*

Whilst pondering warming moments ... I mentioned earlier a dislike of the way social media is used in some situations. However, it can be brilliant for keeping in touch with family and friends, remembering friends' birthdays, bringing people together and match-making ... actually, yes. There's a personal tale of two friends whom I've known for years, Janice Watson and Simon Kenyon-Smith – two lovely people. I've worked with Janice many times over the years, and Simon and I first met when I was playing the organ in Huddersfield Town Hall for a broadcast. Simon is also an organist, though on that particular occasion we were discussing our mutual interest in caving – he's rather more professional than I am. They are both friends of mine on Facebook, but they had also crossed paths themselves many years ago and lost touch. They both commented on one of my Facebook posts, caught up and are now planning to get married in October (2020)!

I feel privileged to have spent many happy years making a living in this extraordinary profession. To say it was work would be far from the truth – as has frequently been said, it's much more a way of life than a job. Sadly, there have been many occasions when I've been asked to take on projects by people who clearly have no understanding of the profession – viewing it as more of a vocation, and assuming that we have a proper 'day job' lurking magically in the background, thereby justifying little or no fee. True, it's not all about money, but it does help to pay the mortgage and buy food! I remember, not so long ago, being asked to play for a wedding in a very 'smart' west London church by a couple who had asked for an organist recommendation from the London Symphony Orchestra. They were given my number and offered me a fee of £50 for what would have been at least four hours of my time, not allowing for any preparation. I tried to explain the situation, but they simply didn't understand. I ended up by asking them to equate the fee they were offering with what they were paying for the church and choir, but apparently, that was quite different! I also went through a period of being asked to play cocktail music in a wine bar on the south coast on New Year's Eve. No fee but as much free drink as I wanted …

In recent years it has felt that much of the public image of classical music has focused on artists and composers who are from the more popular end of the classical world, as highlighted in the Classic Brit Awards. Some of these artists have been thrust into stardom for the profit enhancement of record companies, promoters and managers. Some look ill at ease – frequently being out of their depth, musically. Once, one such singer even walked out of a *Friday Night* recording, in front of an audience, due to an inability to find the necessary notes. Orchestras are frequently shown rudeness in rehearsal due to poor time-keeping or a reluctance to rehearse. A well-known singer, for whom I had to accompany a solo verse in the RAH, arrived shortly before the end of the rehearsal – I was about to start the introduction when his phone rang. He took the call, left the stage, and we performed the piece in the concert without rehearsal.

Documenting aspects of the past forty years or so has been a fascinating project and, as is the way of such things, the more I've written, the more

Recording Percy Grainger's transcription of Debussy's *Pagodes* with Sir Simon Rattle • Symphony Hall, Birmingham (1996)

I've remembered. Knowing that I was working on this book, several friends and colleagues have kindly reminded me of events, some that the passing of time had erased – a sort of natural healing! I hope that the overriding impression gained from my memories is happy and positive, despite my noting just a few frustrations along the way.

I'm going to finish with some events that have made a particularly lasting impression, the first being in Symphony Hall, Birmingham in December 1996, when I joined the CBSO for a recording session of music by Percy Grainger, conducted by Sir Simon Rattle. First, we recorded *The Warriors* – an extravagant and highly exuberant piece for orchestra with three major piano parts. On this occasion I was joined by the pianists Wayne Marshall and Malcolm Wilson. In the evening a small group of us stayed behind after class to record Grainger's transcription of Debussy's *Pagodes*. This arrangement involves a substantial number of keyboard instruments, including a dulcitone, harmonium and celeste, together with four lidless grand pianos, each with a pianist to hold down the relevant notes. Percussionists were deployed to each piano to strike the strings inside with soft percussion mallets. Simon had carefully worked out exactly how we would best interpret the score, allowing for the shape of the metal frame in a modern piano. This was to be one of those occasions you simply wouldn't forget.

A few years later, in 2002, I was invited to join the London Sinfonietta for a performance of the same work to be conducted by the late Paul Zukofsky in the Queen Elizabeth Hall. I didn't know this gentleman, but I understood that he was a violinist and conductor with a specialism

Pagodes with Elizabeth Burley and Helen Crayford, QEH (2002)

for contemporary music. Unlike Simon Rattle, he had not taken the trouble to consider the practicalities of grappling with the inside of a modern piano, and despite being warned, he was quite dismissive when we told him that due to the shape of the frame, we simply didn't have enough players to access the strings at the right moments. He was distinctly unpleasant to us and, as we left the hall, he was heard to ask the orchestra manager why she couldn't have got some 'better keyboard players'. Without wishing to seem immodest, I should say that the assembled company, led by John Constable, was one of the most experienced teams he could wish to have had – this really was mission impossible. It has been said that orchestral players should never forget that the conductor is their natural enemy! This is nonsense, of course – most are there for the same reason as the players – the common purpose of making music together with a sense of mutual respect and cooperation. However, this gentleman came close to proving the occasional veracity of this sentiment.

I've had the pleasure of making music with the CBSO on many occasions, and another especially memorable concert was their 2018 Prom conducted by Ludovic Morlot. I joined them for the organ part of Lili Boulanger's wonderful setting of Psalm 130 – *Du fond de l'abîme* (*Out of the depths*). I'd not heard much of her music previously, and this piece was extraordinarily beautiful and thought-provoking. All the more so when you realise that she wrote it at the age of twenty-two – just two years before her untimely passing.

There were some out-of-the-ordinary and highly memorable occasions for me with the BBC in the eighties, the first being for Bernstein's Broadway musical *On the Town* with the conductor, Paul Daniel (2000). This involved a substantial period of rehearsals working with the soloists Graham Bickley, Karl Daymond and Brent Barrett, as well as the esteemed Kim Criswell and Sally Burgess. These were most enjoyable performances at the RFH, although slightly challenging, as the orchestra was split in two, in order to make something of a performing area for the singers.

A bit of fun arose in 2006, when BBC One ran a series called *Play It Again,* in which celebrities from all walks of life were encouraged to pick up a musical instrument they had learned in their youth. My friend Malcolm Hicks had to introduce Jo Brand to the RAH organ, and I had to rehearse and perform with Lord Robert Winston, who had relearned the saxophone. This was an extremely happy and interesting morning in his home with charming company.

In 2010, I had an unexpected encounter with the demon barber of Fleet Street, when I turned up for the first rehearsal of *Sweeney Todd* to discover that the Prelude was a substantial organ solo. Even more of a surprise was that the Proms management was expecting me to rehearse at around 7:00am on the morning of the concert if I wanted to play the solo through on the RAH organ. That idea was a non-starter for me, due to the length of the day with a live TV broadcast that night. I was actually very naughty – when the orchestral break came, and the hall was quiet, I simply went for it. I could hear people calling in vain, telling me that I couldn't play, but I persevered, and before life became too difficult I had finished the two-minute solo. Due to the volume of sound that organ can produce, there are very good reasons not to play it when people are in the hall trying to set up, work and talk, but there was no immediate issue at that time, and I felt I'd made the sensible decision. This was a thrilling solo to play, all the more so in that building. Petroc Trelawny, presenting for Radio 3, was sitting in the hall for the rehearsal along with the composer, Stephen Sondheim, and he told me afterwards that when I played the first chord, Sondheim "flew back into his seat" – job done, I felt!

I met and worked with the distinguished Sir David Willcocks twice. What a remarkable man and an idol for so many connected with the world of church and choral music. Our first meeting was for a BBCCO gala concert at the Barbican that he was conducting. In truth, much of the music was likely not in his more usual genre. However, there was a wartime medley that contained a hymn setting complete with an organ introduction. This great man, former director of music at King's College, Cambridge and, latterly, director of the Royal College of Music, was now in his element and even asked me to stay on after the rehearsal to go through this section alone. Whilst this was something of a pleasure, I was running short of time to get anything to eat. Although by now Sir David was on a roll, I felt that I had to excuse myself after a further ten minutes of 'instruction'. "Ah, of course," he said. "You an Academy chap?" "Yes," I said. "Ah … " he replied and wandered off, as though that had explained everything!

The second time we met was for a 'come and sing' performance of Rossini's *Petite Messe Solennelle* in the church of Santa Maria Maggiore in Rome (2007). This is an interesting concept whereby people can turn up for the rehearsal of a work and then give a performance later in the day. I was playing the colourful harmonium part, and Jane Watts was playing one of the two pianos. It was all going very well until the rehearsal break, when my bag was stolen from under the piano while I was distracted with a question about the evening's performance. I lost my wallet but luckily, not my passport. After the rehearsal, Sir David came over to commiserate. We chatted for a while, and I asked him about the legendary recordings of the *Psalms of David* he made with the choir of King's College, in 1968. I was fascinated to learn that these had come about by chance – the choir had been prepared to record something completely different, but the soloist was indisposed at the last moment. EMI was already set up and Christopher Bishop, the producer, had asked whether there was anything else they could record. Sir David said that the only practical option for a full-length recording would be the *Psalms*, which were always in their repertoire. He accompanied the choir from the organ loft and the rest is history. Back in Rome, the performance proceeded as planned, and during the interval Sir David chose, rather curiously, to remain standing in his place on the rostrum whilst everyone else left for refreshments!

One of the great joys in life is playing piano-duet recitals with my wife, Jo. Back in 2008, I wrote a piece for piano-duet and orchestra called *Paper Dances*, which was my first (paper) anniversary gift for Jo. We

Recording *Paper Dances* • BBCCO, Southbank Sinfonia, Jo, Stephen Bell and Neil Varley • Radio 3 • Watford Colosseum (Sept. 2008)

recorded this for the BBC and also broadcast it live as part of a *Friday Night* (September 2008) with our friend Stephen Bell conducting and Aled Jones presenting the show. Much of this was written whilst we were on holiday in 2008, no doubt to the chagrin of my wife, although she didn't show it!

We play together in recital as often as possible. Many of our recital programmes have a more classically based first half, with a lighter mood for the second half, frequently including something by two of our favourite composers, York Bowen and Philip Lane. Philip has become a good friend over the years – he makes frequent appearances as a producer on recording sessions, and he has a substantial and highly regarded catalogue of compositions, arrangements and film score reconstructions. For reasons I don't remember, Jo invariably plays primo (the top end) and I, secondo, (down the bottom). They both have their own challenges – the upper part seems to generally have quite a few more notes and also that strange feeling of (usually) not being in control of the pedal. Most usually, the top player manages the page turns to avoid mid-air collisions. Conversely, the lower part doesn't get to play the tunes so often, and also has the challenge of pedalling for someone else. There's another book to be written about the fun and games involved in duet playing – especially if you go back to Mozart, who very much enjoyed the medium of the duet and the opportunities it gave him to get close to some of his young lady pupils!

Sometimes we have the pleasure of playing either piano-duet or two pianos in an orchestral context, such as for *Carmina Burana*, Saint-Saëns' *Organ Symphony* or, as in late 2008, Benjamin Britten's *Saint Nicolas* cantata, for which we joined the BBCCO in a snowbound Lancing College. This performance was expertly piloted by conductor, Paul Brough, mentioned earlier in connection with the Requiem Mass for Dr John Birch.

Rehearsing the *Organ Symphony* with the CBSO in the CBSO Centre, Birmingham (April 2018)

For several years, Jo and I have been the official accompanying pianists for the Harry Mortimer Prize – a solo award organised by the National Youth Brass Band of Great Britain. This involves us in a very happy couple of days in Repton School on the band's summer course, in the company of some quite extraordinarily gifted and delightful young musicians. Bramwell Tovey, greatly respected for his work in the field of brass bands, is artistic director of the NYBBGB.

I reach the end of these reminiscences in the middle of May 2020 amid the terrible pandemic of COVID-19, which has resulted in us being under lockdown for more than two months. A very few restrictions have now been lifted, but some people are, understandably, getting restless and defying this imposition. One can only hope that their, seemingly, reckless actions don't come at a cost for the majority. The future for the entertainment profession seems bleak. Theatres and concert halls are closed, and any discussion of their opening comes with requirements for social distancing, which would mean that to observe the required two-metre distancing between audience members, a venue could only accommodate up to around twenty per cent capacity, making productions financially unviable. The 2020 Proms are unlikely to go ahead, at least not in any form that we would recognise. Let's hope that we can trust the judgement of those in authority to make the right decisions and bring us through this. I feel so sorry for our son and others of his generation, who will be suffering the consequences of this nightmare for many years to come.

Music is a truly international language – wherever you are in the world, it can communicate. Through music you have the power to move people and create emotions, no matter what the genre might be. Music is an extraordinary force for good, and I do feel sad at the progressive cutbacks that the profession has endured in recent years, especially in the area of education. It seems to me that too many people, especially those in a position of power, totally fail to appreciate the value of the arts, both for the soul and the intellect. There have been countless tests showing a correlation between music and brain development, especially in younger children. I frequently think back to the golden period between the late sixties and early eighties that so many of our local musicians experienced in Redbridge, due to the foresight of Malcolm Bidgood and the supportive local council. These cuts, and the consequential loss of investment, have resulted in so many young people not getting these life-enhancing opportunities. We were lucky.

I've heard it said more than a few times that there are only two aspects to a musician's work – either you're bored to death, or you're scared to death! Whilst I can understand facets of each of those statements, this has not been my overriding experience. The road has had a few minor potholes and, to be honest, I would have preferred that those potholes came with a little more courtesy, especially from some management colleagues who don't always stop to consider sensibilities – musicians are not just commodities, and we have feelings! However, so far, it's been an amazing journey – I have played wonderful music with many leading orchestras and conductors; I've visited places that I would probably otherwise never have been able to visit (though usually with not much time to explore), and I have a wonderful, supportive and very long-suffering family – I've been very, very lucky. Never underestimate the consequences of a sneeze ...

Thank you if you planned to read a little from the top and kept going! As for the question you've been holding onto since the beginning – the answer John Birch always gave was, "Because it doesn't need 10,000 pipes!"

With Aled Jones following the broadcast of *Paper Dances*, *Friday Night is Music Night*, Mermaid Theatre (2015)

Piano duet recital, St Patrick's Cathedral, Dublin (2017)

Photographs

Abbreviations

ABRSM	Associated Board of the Royal Schools of Music
BBCCO	BBC Concert Orchestra
BBCSO	BBC Symphony Orchestra
BBCTV	BBC Television
CBSO	City of Birmingham Symphony Orchestra
CCF	Combined Cadet Force
CLS	City of London School
ECO	English Chamber Orchestra
GSMD	Guildhall School of Music and Drama
LPO	London Philharmonic Orchestra
LSO	London Symphony Orchestra
NCO	Non-Commissioned Officer
NYBBGB	National Youth Brass Band of Great Britain
QEH	Queen Elizabeth Hall
RAH	Royal Albert Hall
RAM	Royal Academy of Music
RCM	Royal College of Music
RFH	Royal Festival Hall
RPO	Royal Philharmonic Orchestra
RYC	Redbridge Youth Choir
RYO	Redbridge Youth Orchestra

Other References

Roderick Elms' website can be found at www.masterkeyboards.co.uk. Here you can find full details of his music and CDs.

You can also find videos of his music on his Youtube channel as well as Facebook – search roderickelmsmusic.

His music is published by Camden Music www.camdenmusic.com and distributed by Spartan Press Ltd. www.spartanpress.co.uk. Here his music can be purchased as well as through regular music shops and online outlets.

Index

www.ingramcontent.com/pod-product-compliance
Lightning Source LLC
Chambersburg PA
CBHW040412110426
42812CB00033B/3363/J